LOOKING BACK

A REFLECTION OF LIFE AND FUTURE AHEAD

Arthur W. Hoffmann, Ed.D., P.E.

LOOKING BACK
A REFLECTION OF LIFE AND FUTURE AHEAD

iUniverse books may be ordered through booksellers or by contacting:

iUniverse
1663 Liberty Drive
Bloomington, IN 47403
www.iuniverse.com
1-800-Authors (1-800-288-4677)

Because of the dynamic nature of the Internet, any web addresses or links contained in this book may have changed since publication and may no longer be valid. The views expressed in this work are solely those of the author and do not necessarily reflect the views of the publisher, and the publisher hereby disclaims any responsibility for them.

Any people depicted in stock imagery provided by Getty Images are models, and such images are being used for illustrative purposes only.
Certain stock imagery © Getty Images.

ISBN: 978-1-5320-5305-4 (sc)
ISBN: 978-1-5320-5306-1 (hc)
ISBN: 978-1-5320-5304-7 (e)

Library of Congress Control Number: 2018909176

Print information available on the last page.

iUniverse rev. date: 08/09/2018

INTRODUCTION

Six decades ago a life-changing event occurred that would have a profound effect on my life, legacy and the Hoffmann family heritage. The effect of this avenge would pursue me for many years, far into the future. It has been a haunting memory!

Looking back on the many life events and experiences is a soul-searching endeavor.

I believe that for everyone, there comes a time in life for reflection of one's past and wonder of the future beyond. The past is known but the whole "journey' is not yet complete. For many their legacy has not been immortalized. Hopes, dreams and regrets remain. For this reason it is appropriate for a person to mentally review how and why they arrived at this critical junction in life's travel. You can't change or rewrite the past, but you can have an impact on how you continue the trip. Therefore, a person's autobiography is an essential component of the legacy they leave for future generations to understand and appreciate their heritage. It is the story of a person's life and meaningful events and **memories of their journey through time.**

Therefore the purpose of this book is to share with my many family members, life-long friends and future generations, my memories, major events, thoughts and regrets that I have experienced over many years. It is my hope that readers will understand the circumstances surrounding events and decisions that were encountered and therefore appreciate their heritage and strive to excel in their future endeavors.

This was the era of the Great Depression. Hope was only a dream for many. My parents, George and Amanda Theresa Hoffmann were German immigrants who had come to America to seek freedom, opportunity and employment in the years following World War I and the coming Great Depression. In the early thirties, jobs were scarce and unemployment was rampant throughout the country. Desperate for work, many people and families were attracted to Detroit, where the automobile industry offered some hope of successful employment. George and Theresa were among them.

George Hoffmann, Sr.

My dad grew-up in Magdeburg, Germany. He was one of 6 children. The Hoffmann family owned a German trucking company and were well known in their community. As the 2nd World War proceeded, the Russian army overran that part of Germany and their family and much of the community fled from the Russian carnage; taking with them only the keepsakes they could carry. Most of the family relocated in the small town of Lorrach, Germany on the Swiss border. This would give them swift-access to neutral Switzerland, if necessary to avoid the danger of Nazi or partisan militia action.

This is where many of dad's relatives now live. Lorrach is in a unique location with the train station located in the city of Basel, Switzerland and shared with German connections. This area of Europe is referred to as the four corners by travelers, due to the intersection of Switzerland, France, Germany and the Rhine river valley. It is also close to the Black Forest area of Germany and the Coo-coo clock industry.

Many of our family members and I have visited dad's relatives over the years,where they once owned a café and housing units for the local college students, which allowed us comfortable and convenient accommodation.

My Dad left home as a young teenage boy to find work in the sprawling Hamburg seaport. He began as a cabin boy on a sailing schooner. Learning seamanship he became an accomplished sailor. As a merchant marine he sailed on many European and Scandinavian ships as well as the USA merchant fleet. He would tell us exciting stories about his sailing adventures. He actually sailed to ports around the world. This included trips to Spitzbergen and the Arctic Ocean.

Dad's final sailing trip ended when he worked on a U.S. mine sweeping vessel that collided with a live mine exploding, sending shrapnel over the crew. The ship docked in Galveston, Texas and he was transferred to a hospital in New Orleans. With shrapnel imbedded in his skull, he survived and spent 6 months hospitalized in New Orleans. Following his release from the merchant marine service he would never again return to sailing. He did know a pen-pal friend in Detroit that he had been communicating with, so as a new immigrant he headed to Detroit where he hoped to find work in the auto-industry.

Dad was very determined to succeed and his accomplishments are many. My dad spoke and wrote impeccable German as well as several Scandinavian languages as well as English. His cursive writing script exhibits craftsmanship and perfection. He was always well-liked and easily made friends.

Arriving in Detroit he did not have a job or skilled trade. However, meeting and making German friends who worked in the auto-industry they recommended him as a good candidate willing to learn a trade. He was hired as an apprentice millwright in the tool room of an auto-plant and enrolled at Cass Technical School. He spent evenings and weekends learning math and science and received very good grades. After completing his apprenticeship he became a journeyman tool & die maker.

Dad was very proud of being German and of his heritage. He was well versed in German and European history, especially the significance of Martin Luther and his contribution to the Reformation and the various denominations. While he grew up as a Catholic in his German family he would later join Epiphany Lutheran Church located near Palmer Woods in Detroit. I believe he was very grateful to Rev. E.T. Bernthal the Pastor, because of his devotion and prayers for me when I almost died of "whooping" cough in the hospital in Detroit. Thankfully, I recovered and our family considered Epiphany Lutheran to be our home church for many of our future activities, Sunday school, scouting, baseball and other events.

<u>Amanda Theresa Sorger</u>

My Mom also led an interesting life as a young girl growing-up in a German community that was partitioned after the war and became part of what is now Leipe, Poland. Mom came from a large family with her older-sister and two-brothers, William (Bill) and Arthur (my namesake). Both of the brothers (my uncles) immigrated to Canada in the 30's. Uncle Art settled in Winnipeg and Uncle Bill wound-up in Calgary, Alberta. Bill established the Vulcan Flour Mill. It became well known for its premium bread/ biscuit flour. Vulcan products were sold in both Canada and the U.S. I can remember seeing Vulcan Flour in grocery stores in Detroit. Mom and Sister Wanda (my Aunt) immigrated to Canada and later to the U.S. also at about the same time.

Initially in the U.S., Mom settled in northern Michigan working as a live-in cook and culinary manager for the Crapo family. Henry Howland Crapo was the 14th Governor of Michigan and a lumber baron, owning the largest private lumber firms in Michigan. Crapo was also the president of the Flint-Pere Marquette railroad. His daughter, Rebecca, married William Clark Durant and their only son was William Crapo Durant (Billy Durant) founder of General Motors. They lived in Palmer Woods, an exclusive neighborhood on the outskirts of Detroit. This is the family Mom worked for. She was in-charge of the day-to-day household budget as well as being their personal chef & cook.

In the early days of the booming automobile industry, the elite families would vacation, traveling by automobile caravans to resorts located on the East Coast. Their household staff would accompany them. For the staff this was like a mini-vacation traveling to famous destinations such as Greenbrier, West Virginia, the Biltmore, and other exciting places and being paid for their services.

Theresa (her preferred name) was in a very envious position during the height of the recession. Mom and Dad had met at German-Polish picnics and dances where they became friends. Mom was a great dancer and enjoyed the picnics with the loud band and accordion playing polka & waltz music.

Jobs in Detroit were scarce and the unemployed would gather in downtown Detroit at Grand Circus Park, hoping to get a day-to-day job. This was essentially general-labor jobs such as maintenance or restaurant help.

Knowing that George and his unemployed friends were destitute she would invite them to come-over (clandestine) to Palmer Woods for leftovers from the family dinner. George and friend walked from downtown Detroit to Palmer Woods, approx. 3 miles every evening for the free dinner. Mom was an outstanding cook and I remember her meals and still miss them. Dinner-time was always very special to our whole family. Sunday dinner was especially important and we all looked forward to this event. No one missed this Sunday custom.

Mom was also a culinary expert having unique skills and recipes. Every year Mom entered samples of her canning in the Michigan State Fair. She always won 1st place for her red raspberries and tomato juice recipe that included a fresh parsley-flavor from our garden. I still copy her recipe today and it is a family hand-me-down that my sisters and daughter Kim (and granddaughter Abigail) also make and relish this delightful treat. Her favorite recipes were published in the Michigan State Fair annual winners' cook-book.

Thinking about Mom's cooking reminds me of all the time I spent in the kitchen observing and helping. She sent me on close-by errands to the butcher shop and order 16 pork-chops, telling George the butcher to make sure they were center-cut & fat trimmed. Or I went to the C.F. Smith market for perfect-size baking potatoes. Mom also taught me how to make Swedish pancakes; that I still do today. These pancakes were the rave of the family at breakfast. Because these large pan-size treats were made one-at-a-time we had to scamper for them or miss-out and wait for the next batch to be cooked.

Often for Sunday dinner mom would also bake stuffed pigeon's (called squabs) for each of us, with all of the trimmings. Dad of course raised the pigeons on a special grain menu to help compete in the bird-racing venues.

Another memory comes to mind when I think of mom's cooking. Our favorite place to go out for a great meal was the Dakota Inn Rathskeller in Detroit on John R Street (near 6 mile road). They offered all of the popular German recipes that remind you of Europe. The Rathskeller is like eating in an original German pub. The atmosphere and décor is beautiful, with the painted wall murals and woodwork. Every weekend they feature a sing-along that includes the "schnitzelbank". It still is a very popular restaurant and we will be going back the next time were in Detroit.

George and Theresa Betrothal

Mom and Dad was a very attractive couple. Having met as German immigrants they had a lot in common. This was the era of the great depression and both of them had migrated to Detroit. Amanda-Theresa came here as a culinary cook employed by a wealthy entrepreneurial-automotive family, while George was an unemployed seaman. They had met at cultural social events and had common friends; and they shared many interests. George was a self-taught person and well-travelled, sailing around-the-world. Even though he was not employed he had enrolled at the Cass Technical High School in Detroit and excelled in math, science and shop practice. Working in the automotive tool & die trade he quickly became an apprentice and a skilled tradesman. In the near future George and Theresa were destined to become my parents. And they were wonderful parents to all of us children.

Side-note: Reminiscing about my parents brings back a lesson I will never forget. As a family we attended Epiphany Lutheran Church in our neighborhood. The Pastor of Epiphany was Dr. E.T. Bernthal and he instilled profound wisdom that has guided my life.

Doctor Bernthal is credited with writing the simple definitions or meanings of the God-Given "Ten Commandments". In reciting these ten rules that God delivered to humanity to live-by, Reverend Bernthal developed a simple interpretation of "What Does This Mean" for each of the 'Commandments'.

Specifically, the "Fifth Commandment"; "Honor your father and your mother, that your days may be long in the land that the Lord your God is giving you". This is the only Commandment that comes with a promise by God and means that you may have a long life on earth if it is followed. When I think of Mom and Dad, I believe that the Fifth Commandment was easy to follow.

The Original Hoffmann Family in the USA

George & Theresa were married in the Lutheran Church on June 9, 1932 during the Depression. They lived in an apartment in the Detroit inner city. Mom continued working in Palmer Woods for the Crapo family. Dad was then working as a tool & die maker in the auto industry. The economy was recovering and Detroit and the auto industry was starting to boom. George, Jr. was the first-born child in the Hoffmann family on June 30, 1934. Shortly after they bought their 1st home and moved to 462 Fernhill located in Detroit's suburban eastside near the State Fair Grounds; close to Palmer Woods where Mom used to live and work. At that time George and Theresa were living in the US as legal immigrants, but not yet U.S. Citizens. At the time of marriage, Dad was a German citizen and Mom had Polish citizenship. In the future they would apply for US Citizenship and had to meet certain resident requirements. On September 22, 1947 they finally received their Certificate of Naturalization and became US Citizens.

I have included this official legal information because it would become part of a very interesting situation in the future that could affect the heritage of several Hoffmann children.

There are six children in our family. In addition to my older brother George Jr., I have two younger sisters, Mary and Elizabeth, followed by two younger brothers Walter and Richard. The Hoffmann family began with Brother George Richard born on June 30, 1934. Arthur Walter born two years later on August 3, 1936 was second. Mary Theresa, the 1st girl arrived October 9, 1940. Sister Elizabeth Elinor's birthday is February 10, 1943. Walter Edward was born on November 25, 1946. Richard Paul, the youngest, was born on May 11, 1948. Our family was mom & dad's pride and joy. All of the siblings were unique in many ways. Each of us would have a special life story to share. I believe that all of these stories and memories would be complementary of our childhood upbringing. In particular I have several memories that are specific to my childhood days.

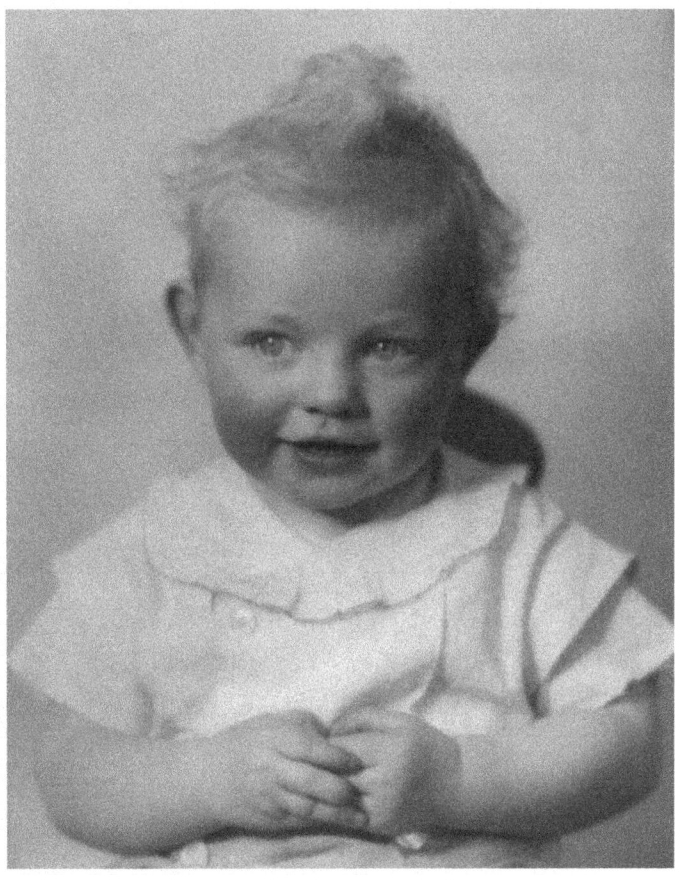

Mom was pleased of her 2nd born. She would like to tell the tale of a neighbor lady walking down the sidewalk while passing our front porch, stopping to see me standing in the playpen and saying, "Arthur, you get cuter every day", and I would answer, "No! Every minute"! Mom would repeat this little tale often while laughing at this jest. I was a happy and playful baby. However, other eventful memories come to mind that are fretful.

When I was about 4 years old I came down with "whooping cough" and nearly died. I was committed to the hospital as an emergency and confined in an oxygen-tent. Pastor Bernthal and my parents would watch over me every day praying for my recovery. I was fortunate for the great medical care and hospital facilities.

Another incident that I vaguely remember was getting hit by a truck as I was running across the street. I only remember looking-up at the bottom of the truck as I lay on the street. The fortunate result was a deep gash on my forehead over my left eye that remains today.

Another mishap occurred due to my stupidity when we kids were playing around a walled-in oil-storage yard. My playmates challenged me to a "dare-you-can't-make-it" event. I leaped from the wall trying to grab-onto an oil-pipe 4 or 5 feet away. Well, I missed, fell down to the ground and broke my left arm and wrist. It still hurts on cold-days.

Growing-Up Memories

During my early childhood we lived in a small frame house, at 462 Fernhill in the eastside of Detroit. Our house was very close to the Michigan State Fair Grounds. The neighborhood was largely inhabited by German / Italian Americans; people with mostly blue-collar occupations.

I attended Grayling Elementary School, which was within walking distance of our home. Bussing was non-existent in those days. Schools were disciplined and teachers' respected. I started kindergarten in September 1941 and can still recall the daily air-raid and fire-drills we had at school after Pearl Harbor on December 7, 1941. My childhood memories are of war games and ration lines for gas, bubble-gum and chocolate.

During the war years Detroit neighborhoods were subject to a lights-out order and there was a patrol officer that walked the sidewalks to ensure that it was followed. As children we were given picture cards of various Japanese airplanes or fire-balloons that we should keep under continuous an observation. Actually, in California some of these armed balloons were actually discovered.

Following Pearl Harbor and the U.S. entry into the now World War II, our neighborhood was subject to U.S. government search and seizure due to the concern that German and Italian citizens may have allegiance to the enemy or spying. I recall the police or military officers entering and searching our house. They were confiscating any guns, large knives and any potential weapons. Our RCA floor model radio was equipped with AM, FM and a Short Wave circuit. They dismantled the "short-wave", but left the AM so we could still listen to the "Lone Ranger". Dad was given a receipt for the so-called "contraband". Following the war, Dad and I went to the Palmer Park police station to retrieve some of the items. They showed us room-after-room, filled to the ceiling with the tagged-seized-items. And this was only a small part of the "contraband"; there were also off-site warehouses with additional stuff. It would be impossible to find your items. Growing-up in the war years was indeed a real-life learning experience that would determine a person's generational values and future life decisions.

Another especially interesting experience was our visits to see the Italian prisoners that were housed within the Michigan State Fairgrounds during World War II. These were all educated officer-class men that were captured and transferred to the U.S. to isolate them from further combat in Europe.

They worked in the wood-shop and gardens, made toys, birdhouses and trinkets that they exchanged for sausage, cookies and homemade food made by the many Italian women who visited daily. Following the war many of these persons became permanent immigrants and valuable citizens.

As I reflect about my childhood days and the entertainment available within our neighborhood; it was a fairly simple life. Games such as kick-the-can, hide-and-seek, marbles and rubber-band gunfights were self-organized and managed. We played sandlot baseball, choosing teams was accomplished by a bat toss gripping the bat in a hand-over-hand dual (no eagle-claws allowed) for closest to the rim. Organizations such as Little-League teams were unknown. Children were independent and self-sufficient.

Toys were few and many were hand-made out of wood and tin. Single speed fat-tire bicycles were the only type available and popular brands were Schwinn and Roadmaster, sold largely at Sears-Roebuck or Montgomery Wards. Children repaired their own bikes, changing tubes, tires and chains.

Reading and trading comic books was also a popular pastime; especially the popular Classic Comic label series of "true-life" story heroes such as Daniel Boone, Kit Carson or the Lone Ranger and U.S .historic events. Playing marbles was also popular on the school playground. The only thing required was a bag of marbles and a circle, scratched in the ground (large or small diameter based on skill). The winner collected and kept the loser's marbles. Trading marbles was a pastime and the larger shooter marbles were especially valued.

Building and flying your own kite was a required skill in order to be competitive and able to maneuver the kite and send it higher, with or without a fancy tail. Kite tails were unique and usually made out of rags tied together thru experiment.

Radio was the only medium for listening and enjoying stories about fictional hero characters such as Superman, Batman, Lone-Ranger and mystery sequels. Children would often fall-a-sleep; listening to the scary-stories and spooky sounds.

Stores and shopping were experiences very different from the popular pastime we know today. The corner drugstore and the close-by A&P or CF Smith grocery stores were located in the neighborhood within walking distance. The corner hamburger grill was the only neighborhood eating place. The sweet shop sold ice-cream cones for a nickel and community refrigeration was located in a wood-insulated shed full of large ice-blocks for home delivery. The Sears-Roebuck and Montgomery Wards were the only large department chains available within a mile or two. S.S. Kresge or Woolworth's were popular "five & dime" stores for everyday household items.

This was the era of my upbringing. The late 1930's and World War II 40's would have a profound effect that established our basic values, philosophy and legacy. Future events and progress would always be evaluated relative to the wisdom of past experiences. From early childhood I was determined to work hard to achieve my future goals. Mom and Dad inspired my self-discipline and desire to achieve and succeed in whatever activity I would pursue. Even as a young boy I had to earn my monetary allowance. In those days homes were heated by coal furnaces that required removing the ashes (clinkers). I did this job for an elderly neighbor who would pay me a quarter every week.

My early years are that of family activities and playing in the neighborhood with mostly older kids. This was because of Brother George, who was obligated to watch-over me and follow his directions specifically. If George got into mischief or trouble we were both involved. I was expected to jump-in if George got into a fight and I was always the one to pay the price since other guys were older and bigger.

More than once some of the big boys would try to tie me up to a post or tree to keep me from helping George but my young sister Elizabeth (Liz) would yell and scream to get help. She always looked after me so I wouldn't get hurt. We were a close family and always respected each other.

George and I shared several funny experiences that I vividly remember. The old Detroit neighborhood was located very near to the railroad tracks and we often played around freight cars. On one occasion we were inside a boxcar when the train started-up abruptly, the door closed and by the time we got it open the train was moving at a pretty good clip and very scary. It travelled a good distance before slowing down allowing us a chance at jumping. We rolled down the embankment safely and luckily only had to walk back a mile or so. The train was heading to the next town.

On another occasion George and I went skinny-dipping at the fair-grounds racetrack gravel-pit. When we got out, someone stole or clothes; all of them. We had to return home hiding in the alley behind the street.

Our house on Fernhill had a vacant lot next to it and we used this lot to park cars for people going to the horse races at the State Fairgrounds. Parking was not allowed on the streets so George and I went to the alley outlet at the end of the street with a $1.00 parking sign and waved the cars in. In those days, cars had running-boards, so we took turns standing on the cars directing the driver to our lot. We didn't drive so the cars were parked somewhat hap-hazard. When the drivers paid we told them getting out would not be a problem. After the races George and I would watch the mayhem from our basement grade-level window as the drivers tried to retrieve their cars.

The Fernhill house had a nice-sized backyard that bordered on a conventional alley, where people put-out their trash and garbage. My dad had constructed a small garage-style building that he used as his pigeon coop. It had small side door and also a roll-up door into the alley. The pigeon coop was un-heated and contained bags of bird feed and yard-tool storage. George and I found this little shed to be a life-saver on occasion when we were locked out of the house. In cold weather we had to use this shed to keep warm as we cuddled together while sitting on the bags of bird seed.

Mom was very proud of Sister Mary and as Mary grew-up Mom would take her to tap-dancing lessons or modeling classes after school. Mom always locked our house when she was away and George and I had to stay outside until she returned with Mary. The shed became our refuge place.

I'm sure that Brother George would remember these above episodes and probably many more that we experienced growing-up. Albert Flamme my neighbor and best friend shared experiences playing and adventuring together; often getting into trouble with neighbors and other kids. Al and I lost contact with each other over the years, but many years later we would be re-acquainted (see later).

My Dad also raised homing pigeons and we had pigeon coops at both the Fernhill house and later at the Hawthorne address. Dad belonged to a group of mostly Belgian (European) pigeon breeders that held racing events. The breeders and followers would bet on the outcome of the various races. Breeders and pigeons are ranked by class, and the bird carries a labeled registration ring on their foot. Homing Pigeons always return to their place of birth once they are released to fly. The home location and place of the race starting point are used to calculate the time & distance these homing birds arrive back home and this is documented. Winners can bring the owners a good deal of money due to the betting-odds. Pigeon owners who are planning a long trip (sometimes as much as one hundred miles or more), would meet or call each other to schedule races and wagers. I would go with my Dad whenever we went on vacation or to visit distant friends. A friend or neighbor would always watch for the returning bird and time of arrival. The returning bird would arrive at the garage and be captured in a one-way trap door leading into the coop area. A calculation was made and the contestants would pay the winner. This was a serious hobby, but these pigeon-raisers were longtime friends and enjoyed sport.

This tale also has an interesting ending. My Dad donated several of his champion pigeons to the U.S. Army during the war and they were sent to England for breeding and their offspring used as wartime carrier pigeons. At the end of the war my Dad received a commendation for his contribution to the war-effort.

Looking back, I believe that persons growing up in cities and neighborhoods in 1940s war-years have an ingrained value system and appreciation of the enormous progress that has occurred in relatively only a few years. I remember that this era brought us an accelerated lifestyle due to the invention and development of all sciences, electricity, transportation, refrigeration, manufacturing, production, airlines, and communication that has been non-stop. The simple life has disappeared. As I grew-up we still had house-to-house delivery of milk (by horse & carriage), door-to-door salesmen, ice delivery, front streets and alleys for trash and parking. Actually when this house was built the kitchen was designed with a wall-opening to slide-in the Frigidaire that had been recently invented by General Motors. The Frigidaire trade name became common for referring to future refrigerators in general.

Another memory and simple attraction was the long-forgotten "scheenie" man that drove thru the alleys on his horse-drawn wagon picking-up useful trash and buying rags or other items that the neighbors had for sale, He would sound his blow-horn to alert potential customers of his passing. This is just a funny memory that younger persons are probably unaware of; but it was a very common event and demonstrates the progress the economy has made over a short period of time.

<u>Our New Family Home</u>

Following World War II in 1946 we moved to another close-by Detroit neighborhood. The home we moved into was a very nice large brick house with an extra adjacent lot that was fully fenced-in. The address was 19457 Hawthorne in Detroit near what is now the I-75 freeway, between7 & 8 mile roads. This house also had a 2-car garage that Dad converted into an overhead pigeon-coop. This is the place that was the home for his newly-bred racing pigeons.

Another memory I reflect on, is my Dad's small workshop in our basement that had a shoemakers' fixture and tools. In those days it was common to re-sole leather shoes for the whole family. In this little shop I discovered a way to make money; actually, just nickels. I would make a hinged wood press and then insert a real nickel (heated red-hot using the hot-water tank burner) into the wood-press, squeeze-together burning the nickel impression into the wood form. When the form cooled I would melt solder into the mold to form a fake nickel. After polishing the nickel with a thick rag I was able to spend-it in a popcorn or candy machine that was available in many places.

I was always interested in woodworking and my dad bought me a small jig-saw for Christmas one year at Sears. It was my favorite hobby to make all-sorts of plywood shelves with elaborate cut-out decorations. My mom would hang them up and put her little nick-knacks on them. I still have few of these shelves and the original jig-saw that I still use for cut-outs on projects I work on.

Youth and Teenage Activities

As George and I grew-up we played sandlot baseball and football together. George became very interested in baseball as a pitcher. I of course became the catcher. George studied the art of pitching so intensely that he could become a pro. I had to catch all manners of pitches he was practicing; fastballs, curves, sliders, knuckleballs, etc. Baseball became more than a sport for us.

George and his friend discovered an opportunity for earning money by working for the ushers at Tiger Stadium. We made an acquaintance with the main usher and he agreed to let us in early sneaking-in thru the over-head sliding door. Our job was to help seat the upper level customers find & wipe their seats (for tips); thus the name rag-boys for this part-time job. We also got to watch the baseball and football games in the best unoccupied seats for free.

As a family we continued to attend Epiphany Lutheran Church and I had perfect attendance in Sunday school over several years. George and I were both in the children's choir. Problem was I'm tone deaf. The choir director instructed me to move my lips without any sound; but I did look good in my robe tough.

My next step was to join the Boy Scouts, Troop #58 at the Epiphany Church. I graduated through the ranks over time and finally achieved Eagle Scout and then Explorer Scout rank. I remember working on all my merit badges for the various skills and knowledge. I still have my merit badge sash and remember how my Mom sewed each one on by hand as well as all my emblems. I'm so lucky and proud of her.

For several years I was a Detroit News carrier boy. At that time you had to buy your route and pay for the papers prior to delivery to the subscriber. Typically, I serviced my route on my bike. After paying for and receiving the papers at the delivery station (a garage) you had to tightly fold them so that you could throw them from the sidewalk onto the customer's front porch. They usually hit the storm door with a bang. Sometimes you had to pay to replace a pane-of-glass. Al Kaline (Tiger pitcher) was one of my customers. The paper route was my first introduction to business.

Also, in those days bowling was a popular sport. Bowling alleys were common in many Detroit neighborhoods. The typical bowling alley was a two-story building because the upstairs housed itinerant workers or homeless men that worked below and set pins for room & board. These pin-setters were supplemented by young boys anxious to make some spending money. I was one of them and worked during evening hours. We were paid 10 cents/line and often worked two-adjacent alleys, jumping back & forth between bowlers of either team. Getting hit by a flying pin was part of the job.

My Education

At our new address on Hawthorne, I attended Nolan Intermediate School, which was just across the street. At that time the Detroit Public School system curriculum for intermediate (middle-school) education included mechanical shop (trade-school) classes as well as commercial & home making skills. Students were taught machine-shop, wood-shop, auto repair and drafting for boys. Girls were taught typing, cooking, domestic & secretarial skills. I learned a great deal in these courses that would prepare me for the future. I believe the same was true for girls. I did like wood-shop class where you could make your own projects. I made several shelves and nick-knack items on the jig-saw. The hardest thing I made was an actual baseball bat, made out of a hardwood pallet log on a large wood lathe. It was held by the two-center points and turned at a slow speed. When I first started the lathe the entire lab shook and vibrated and the instructor went hyper, but eventually it smoothed-down. I actually used the baseball bat but I wish I would have kept it as souvenir.

Hands-on skills such as wood-working, mechanical drafting and engineering became my life-long ambition. Further education and continuous learning was a priority.

Ford Trade School / Pershing High School

Graduation from Nolan Intermediate School led to the next step in my education, growth and maturity. The technical education and training in machine shop and drafting skills led me to consider my future path and livelihood. Typically the student at this time would advance and attend the closest public high school available. For me that was Pershing High School, within a few miles from home. However, I decided to apply for admission to the Henry Ford Trade School in Dearborn, Michigan. I was accepted and began classes in January 1951. Ford trade school was considered a premier technical school that offered skilled employment following graduation. The attendance format was 2-weeks at the academic facility called "Camp Dearborn" and 2-weeks at the Ford Rough assembly plant. At the plant a skilled tradesman would directly supervise the student in the proper technique for the various machines and tooling equipment. The training included blueprint reading, dimensioning and design requirements. The full apprenticeship required 4-years of schooling with a similar amount of actual trade work experience. Learning skills were advanced over the course of the apprenticeship.

We were paid a stipend of $12.00 /week that was paid in cash every 2 weeks. The cash was always counted-out as two $10.00 bills & two $2.00 bills. This was used to pay bus fare and a box lunch at the plant. At the school we received a free hot lunch, but we were assigned to the kitchen and school clean up as part of the discipline.

Unfortunately, Ford Trade School was closed after my 1st year due to the graduates accepting higher-paid positions in the competitive tool/die and design industry.

In January 1952 I transferred to Pershing High School to finish my high school education. Since I was not a freshman at Pershing, I missed the college-preparation-course curriculum and was assigned to the general-ed. course of study. At Pershing I chose to focus on science and drafting as my primary interest of study. At the time I had not decided on attending college full-time because I was interested in becoming a draftsman or designer due to the many opportunities in the auto-industry. I believed that if I got a good job I could pursue an engineering degree through a part-time evening/weekend course of study in the future.

High School & Social Activities

Pershing High was a large school that serviced the lower eastside of Detroit. The student population was primarily 'blue collar', nationality and racially mixed. There was a wide-range of art, music, cultural, and technology opportunities for educational and social activities. It was a typical American high school environment. Football, basketball and sporting events were very competitive and popular. Students formed various groups, gangs and hung-around their favorite soda-shop, deli or pizza place. We did all of the things that young teenagers do prior to maturing. This was mostly for fun and enjoyment but troublesome activities occurred as well. Typically, small groups of friends (boys/girls) would meet and do things in common together. For example both school and organized dances were popular. Casual dating was the primary motivation that bound people together. Serious dating and sex was not a common thing. Going steady was. I was very fortunate to have a nice car to use for driving to and from school. It was Brother George's 1950 Chevrolet convertible; metallic blue color with a white canvas-top. The car was a very useful attraction in making friends, especially girls.

The reason I had use of the car was because George had joined the U.S. Navy Reserve with a friend. They attended several reserve meetings at the Detroit Naval Armory. With the war in Korea in progress George decided to volunteer for the draft and because he was in the naval reserve he was allowed to choose his term or service and location when the Navy released him. George was inducted into the U.S. Army and sent to Camp Picket, Virginia for basic training and then served the remainder of his term in Germany. While in Germany George met and was in contact with our family relatives. I watched-over his 1950 Chevrolet convertible while he was gone from 1951 to 1953.

Life after High School Graduation

Following high school graduation I applied for admission to Wayne State University since my academic grades were very good, but I lacked the college prep experience necessary for admission. They responded that I would be accepted at Wayne State University as trial engineering student. I attended full-time for the 1st semester and was fully accepted due to my 4-point average. While attending Wayne State full-time, I got a job working part time at a gas station, pumping gas, checking oil and washing cars by hand.

The Speedway 79 gas station was located at the busy intersection of James Couzens Ave. and Northwestern Highway in the famous car-cruising corridor. Car traffic was a continuous loop during evening/night hours with all of the drive-in restaurants and cars gassing-up. In between customers I used the downtime for doing my homework. For the coming year I continued working at the gas station and attending Wayne State in the School of Engineering, concentrating on my studies. I continued living at home at the Hawthorne address with our whole family. George as I remember had a job at the Chrysler Highland Park plant and after a while he moved into an apartment in close-by Highland Park. George had attended and graduated from Detroit Commerce High School and studied finance and accounting that prepared him for the job at Chrysler.

The Speedway station was a popular spot for local business customers since the owner allowed regular customers to charge their gas and pay as they could. Among the customers was a company called "Silent Maid". This company sold and installed garbage-grinders, a new product that had about 50 sales people. Their office was adjacent to the station and brought-in a lot of business to us. As a result I was able to do side-chores for these people to help with my tuition and expenses. I cleaned their office and also did minor mechanical repairs.

Friendship, Marriage and Regrets

One evening while on duty at the gas station, a car driven by single gal pulled-in and I pumped her gas and cleaned the windshield as always. We had a short conversation and talked about the many drive-in restaurants and attractions along the highway. Most of restaurants were serve-at-the-car, where the waitress would roller-skate out, take your order and return with the food tray that attached over the driver's rolled-down window. Eating in the car and flirting with boys or girls was the real attraction. It was a continuous loop that lasted all evening until closing. Celine was an attractive lady and I found her interesting to talk-to and very friendly.

A while later; she drove in again; and we had a longer conversation. Her name was Celine and she was single and worked at Michigan Bell Telephone. She lived alone in an apartment close to work. Her dad recently retired from Detroit Edison and her parents had bought a small farm in Auburn, Michigan near Midland and had recently moved there. Because of her good job she decided to remain in Detroit. She had a number of friends and fellow workers to support her. We had a nice conversation and she would stop in again the next time she was cruising. Well I was anxious to see her again and she did stop-by several other times to talk. On one such occasion she asked me out for coffee after I closed the shop. She would visit me at the station regularly and we advanced from coffee to movies and beyond.

After dating a while she wanted me to meet her parents at their farm in Auburn, Michigan and we planned a weekend trip. My parents knew that I was dating Celine but they had not met her at that time. When I told my mom that I was taking the weekend trip, she was upset since I had never missed our mandatory Sunday family dinner.

However, I did make the trip and met Celine's mom and dad. We had separate sleeping arrangements at the farmhouse. In the future there would be several more visits.

During one of the visits her dad scheduled a "barn-raising" on his farm. Typically friends and neighbors' joined in the construction of the new barn and a cook-out ceremony afterwards. The most difficult part of the project was raising the side wall frames and tying them together to form the roof structure. Since I was a young man I agreed to be one of the raising crew (about 3/side). This meant climbing the highest extension ladders and bolting the trusses together while hanging-on and not falling 40 or more feet to the ground. It was successful but not a fun visit.

On another trip to visit to see her parents at the farm in Auburn we had an auto accident. A man ran a red light and crashed into the passenger's side of our 1948 Dodge sedan. We had to sue the driver for damages to our car and that required hiring an attorney I knew. He was an acquaintance from my days at the gas station. He pursued our case and settlement. He would later represent me in another legal action.

A most memorable visit to the farm was the return of Celine's family's from a month-long vacation trip to Montreal, Canada. When Celine returned I was shocked to learn that she may be pregnant. She was unsure of the timing and we discussed the options. I did not know what to do and how to inform my family. We decided to just let them know that we were planning to get married; but not in a church ceremony.

Celine and her good friends, Orville and Geraldine made arrangements and stood-up for us to get married at the county court house. The date was August 19, 1955. This was just over 1 year since I graduated from high school. My mom and dad were upset by our decision; but I'm certain they knew the reason. It was the hardest thing I ever did!

To demonstrate how gracious they were; my mom invited us to dinner following the in-court wedding. My parent's house had a finished basement that had a downstairs kitchen. This is where we had our wedding dinner that mom prepared. It was a private dinner with only mom, dad, Celine and me. George, Mary and Sister Elizabeth were not invited. After dinner we discussed our future and they wished us well, but it was not a happy occasion. Mom also presented us with a complete set of "Revere Ware" as a gift.

We then went "home" to her friend's house in Garden City where they offered us an attic bedroom. It was a brand new small ranch style house that they had recently moved into. The attic was unfinished and we found-out that wood sap was dripping down onto the new bedroom set Celine had recently purchased. My first maintenance job was to line the rafters with cardboard from broken move-in boxes. While we lived in her friends' home I helped him with the landscaping, sodding grass and other maintenance chores.

Orville was a heating duct installer and because of my drafting and mechanical experience I designed a system to help him quote prospective jobs. This blueprint template depicted a typical house floor plan showing the joists layout and floor structure required to fit and run the heating ducts to scale with dimensions. All a contractor needed to do was to highlight the design of the required system, label the parts, add the specific installation time and cost for the job quote. This became very useful to him or for any other contractor.

After living in the attic and helping out, I was surprised to learn that Celine was paying her friend weekly rent for our accommodations. We decided to move to an apartment flat on the eastside of Detroit near her work. The only furniture we had was the bedroom suite that Celine had purchased at a small furniture store near the farm in Auburn, Michigan. She was very pleased with this bedroom set since it was the only possession we owned. My mom and dad came to visit us one time at this upstairs apartment and we had to sit on milk-crates in the front room. Celine continued working at Michigan Bell and I was still working at the gas station.

However during this period I quit my job at the gas station. I had applied for an apprentice job opening in a small tool shop. They hired me on a temporary basis because of my experience at Ford Trade School and my ability to layout a machining design using a digital height gage and micrometer. Since my dad was a tool/die-maker, he gave me a nice tool chest and necessary tools needed for my new job. I worked for this small company for a little over a month when they notified me that they had to let me go because they were a union shop and they were not going to allow me to join the union.

Fortunately I was able to find a job right away as a junior draftsman and blueprint machine operator at Jervis B. Webb a large assembly-line equipment company. However I continued to seek other job positions within the auto-industry and applied for several openings listed in the newspaper want ads.

After completing my 1st semester toward an engineering degree at Wayne State I decided that instead of continuing full-time college I would rather find a better paying job. I felt that if I could find a job such as a detail draftsman and then over time I could become a product designer. I would then complete my engineering degree attending evening or weekend courses. That was always my plan and it did materialize in the distant future.

My big break came in October 1955, when I got a call from the General Motors Ternstedt Division that they wanted to interview me. They were starting a junior drafting school program and I could be a candidate provided I passed a competency test. I interviewed well, passed the test and I was hired. The GM Ternstedt Division designed and manufactured most of the mechanical hardware for all GM vehicles as well as for a number of competitors. Our apprentice drafting group consisted of about 12 people and we were supervised by other senior designers. It was the best job I could have imagined. We were paid well and regularly scheduled for overtime with pay. We could now afford a nicer apartment and moved to a rental flat near my parents' house.

An Unexpected Divorce

Baby Arthur was born on April 10, 1956. Celine, of course, was not working at that time and we continued to live in the upstairs flat near my parents. It was a mostly Polish-Italian neighborhood on the eastside of Detroit. A while after Arthur Jr. was born Celine had contact with a priest from the Catholic Church in our neighborhood. The purpose was to discuss baby Arthur's baptism.

We had never discussed any religion and I was unaware that she apparently was a devout Roman Catholic and her parents even more so. She asked if I would go to a meeting with the priest to discuss the process. Since I was not Catholic and we were not married in the Church it apparently presented some problems. I met with the priest on two occasions. Celine was not part of the discussion. The priest explained baptism within the Catholic Church and my role for the future religious upbringing and education of Arthur Jr. I told him I was in favor of baptism since I was brought-up in the Lutheran Church and I would like for the baby to be baptised in either the Catholic or the Lutheran Church. However, I was not willing to allow someone else other than Celine or me to determine our son's educational future.

At the 2nd meeting the priest presented me with some papers to review and sign. Essentially, the papers stated that the church has chosen a couple from their congregation that agreed to oversee and assure that Arthur Jr. would be brought-up in the Roman Catholic faith and education following the baptism, until his 18th birthday. Furthermore, I would give-up all rights or privileges to interfere with this process. I read this agreement and told him I definitely would not agree to this church policy. The priest reacted with anger calling me evil and without redemption. I went home and explained the situation with Celine. I told her I would be glad to have the baby baptised anywhere, but I just can't sign those papers. It was not a happy ending.

After a short period of time I returned home from work one evening to find Celine and the baby missing. I found out that her dad had picked them up and brought them to the farm in Midland.

I was alone that evening when there was a knock at the apartment door. I opened the door and a man was there and he asked if I was Arthur Hoffmann, I replied yes, and he handed me an envelope and said "you have been served" and left down the stairs. I was dumbstruck. I opened the document that was a subpoena requiring me to appear in divorce court. I did not know what to do; so I called Mr. Coleman, the lawyer that handled our auto accident case. I explained everything to him and he said he would look into situation. A day or so later he called and told me this was "an-open & shut-case". He told me the Catholic Church sponsored the motion, the judge was chosen and the divorce would occur on the court date. He would be present to represent me to ensure that I would get fair treatment.

The divorce court date was May 21, 1957. After I arrived I was told that I would have to wait outside of the actual courtroom. While I was waiting, Celine entered the courtroom, without acknowledging me. After it was over she left without saying anything.

The whole process was very distressful. The "divorce decree" states that Celine was given total custody of the child. I was ordered to pay child support until the child reached his eighteenth birthday. I was allowed visiting rights to see the baby at Celine's home at reasonable (periodic) times and hours by appointment. Arthur Jr. was 13 months old at that time. To this day, it is difficult to mentally reconstruct how this it all happened.

Life Following the Divorce

After the divorce, Celine went back to her old job at Michigan Bell and moved to an apartment close-by my parents. My mom agreed to care for the baby during the day and Celine would drop-off and pick-up Arthur as long as Celine continued to work. I lived in the same house but I was working over-time hours and she and I rarely crossed-paths. My mom of course became very attached to the baby over time. I did visit the baby at her apartment several times, but was limited to one-hour. Celine was very distant like we were strangers. After a couple of months Celine quit her job and moved to the Westland area. She did not contact me that she had moved and I was unable to contact her. I had to get her contact information from the Friend of the Court where I was sending my child support payments.

I called her to arrange an appointment to visit the baby. My mom and sister Mary went with me to her new address that turned out to be a very small ranch-type house close to the Detroit-Wayne airport. It was a fairly long drive from the eastside of Detroit, especially before I-94 was completed. We did visit baby Art and I remember him barely walking then. We brought some new toys for him and the visit lasted about one hour. Celine did not join us, but stayed elsewhere in the house.

A month or so later I called to make another appointment and to my shock and surprise she informed me that she had gotten remarried and in the future I had to deal with her new husband for scheduling my visits. I let her know that I was going to contact the Friend of the Court because this was a violation of the divorce decree.

I also told her it has been a long time since I saw Arthur and I was planning to come out there next Sunday afternoon, same as the last time. I did make this visit but it was very uncomfortable. I went alone and her husband let me in and we sat in the small front room, with him in a chair watching me. Arthur played on the floor with his toys. Celine was in another room of the house and refused to see me. *(Actually, I would never see her again, except for an unusual future occurrence that I will explain later).*

Going forward, I tried to contact Celine numerous times. There was never an answer to my calls or messages. After a period of time my mom, Sister Mary and I decided to drive out to Westland on a Sunday afternoon to see how Arthur Jr. was doing. There was no answer when we rang the bell or knocked on the front door. The house appeared to be vacant. I went over to the next-door neighbor's house and explained our visit. They said that the family had moved out. The neighbor believed that they moved to California, but had no idea where. I contacted the Friend of the Court and they had no further information. She had not notified them that she had moved at all; and especially out of Michigan. I had no way of finding them personally and I did not want to hire a detective or pursue it any further. It was obvious that she and her new husband did not want me in the picture. My parents often asked about Arthur. Over the years I often thought about Art, Jr., worried and prayed often that all was well with him. In later years my prayers would be answered.

New Job Offer - Chrysler Defense Operations

I had completed my drafting training at GM-Ternstedt and hopeful of a permanent position at the new GM Technical Center in Warren, Michigan. However, we were notified that only a small number of the current employees would be eligible for transfer to the new facility. I was very concerned about losing my job, especially at this time. As a result I applied for an opening at Chrysler Defense Operations in Centerline, Michigan and I was hired in April 1958

This engineering and design department was part of the Chrysler Military Tank Group. As a draftsman I specifically worked on the design of military tank body and turret structure. Overtime as I gained experience I was promoted to more advanced projects. One of the projects was the design of a new all-aluminium light truck designed to have air-lift and drop capability.

As an employee of Chrysler Defense Engineering I was able to attend evening classes at the Chrysler Institute of Engineering at the Highland Park Campus. These were advanced technology courses taught by Chrysler Engineering staff professors in their masters' program. Chrysler Engineering was highly-recognized for advanced research and automotive innovation. My course work at Chrysler Institute proved to be very beneficial for my future career.

A Second Marriage

I continued working for Chrysler Defense Operations Division in Warren, Michigan and did very well advancing to higher positions in the design of military tanks and vehicles. During this time I had met and started dating one of my sister Mary's friends. Her name was Delores and she also lived in our neighborhood. We got along very well and after a year of dating we decided to get married. In this case we discussed religion and she was not committed to any particular church or denomination. She agreed to attend my Lutheran Church and go to group classes explaining our basic beliefs. On September 6, 1958 we got married in that church and had a good size wedding reception at a local banquet hall. I had a good job and she was not employed except for a short-term job as a clerk or sales. We moved into an apartment in the neighborhood and spent most of our spare time with our mutual friends.

I continued working at Chrysler Defense and got several promotions as I gained experience and also completed advanced technical courses at Chrysler Institute of Engineering in Highland Park, Michigan. My work assignments grew more difficult and involved original design projects for specific military tank features such as under-water fording ; ability of a tank to cross a water hazard. I also worked on the design of the advanced M-60 tank that had several unique features.

The U.S. Army and Korea

In August 1959 I received official notification that I was selected (drafted) for military service. Following the mandatory physical at Detroit Fort Wayne, I was inducted on August 27, 1959 and immediately sent (by train) to Fort Leonard Wood, Missouri, for basic training.

After 16 weeks of basic I was eligible for leave and home for the Holidays. Returning to Fort Leonard Wood I was assigned as an instructor at their mechanical drafting/engineering school. Fort Leonard Wood is the headquarters for the U.S. Army's Engineering Corps. This involves building bridges, rafts and eliminating obstacles for military manoeuvres.

In March 1960 I was transferred to Fort Hood, Texas, headquarters for the 5th Army Tank Corps. This reassignment was possibly due to my tank design experience. During this whole military period, Delores had moved back home and we communicated by phone or mail.

At Fort Hood I was allowed to live off base and so I rented a small house trailer in a civilian/military complex just outside of the base. I had leave time and I drove to Detroit to pick-up Delores and we lived in this trailer until I was ordered to go to Korea in June 1960 for the duration of my service. Delores returned home and I reported to Oakland, California where I boarded a troop ship to Korea.

I arrived to Korea in June 1960 and was assigned to The 8th Army General Staff and United Nations Command in Seoul, Korea. This UN facility was actually the former Japanese occupation base. The base was fairly large, partially walled and totally fenced. Several 2 or 3 story brick buildings housed the officers' quarters and also served as the clerical offices and General Staff Operations meetings. The remainder of the base housed enlisted personnel, in a maze of Quonset-hut type buildings for the various activities. I was quartered with the other service staff members in one of these buildings.

My job was as a draftsman and map-coordinator. These 3D dimensional maps were about 2 feet square and depicted all aspects of the terrain elements such as elevations roads, bridges, mountain passages and other critical operational information. The maps were assembled much like inter-locking tiles with staples and interlock features. We had maps that covered the entire Korean peninsula, North, South and adjacent ocean or border countries. The maps were updated continuously as required.

Part of my assignment was to also attend the general staff meetings as a map-coordinator. My job was to move or locate operational units and equipment on the 3 dimensional map display and point out potential obstacles, elevations and road/bridge accessibility. It was an interesting experience.

Working in the company office as a draftsman I prepared overhead slides and detailed prints of various maneuver schematics for officer presentations. I actually wrote and published a how-to-do manual for overhead slide preparation. I received a commendation for this work from the General Staff Commander.

During my stay in Korea I made some very good friends in our company and we actually organized a fraternity-type group based on our estimated release date out of Korea (EDS). All of us had technical/engineering background experience. A couple of the members were associated with the U.S. CARE organization dedicated to good works in needy countries. Our group with CARE funding of building materials volunteered to renovate a small dirt-floor school building in the Seoul countryside. We worked over several weekends and added the foundation and full cement floor for the "True Life School", Seoul, Korea in 1961. We were presented an engraved Zippo lighter as a keepsake that I'm very proud of today.

While in Korea I made close friends with Sheigo Matsumara, my upper-bed-mate, who was an American 1st degree judo black belt. He was engaged in learning the Korean version of "judo" by a 3rd degree Korean army instructor. I joined the training class with several other GI's. This on-site training was to reflect combat conditions and personal hand-to-hand manoeuvres. He had a lot of actual and interesting stories to share with us about his recent war experience. I started-out with a trainee white-belt and after a while I achieved blue-belt status. This was a good learning experience but I would not be competitive today.

The 2nd Divorce

Sometime in July/August 1960, I received a call from the company commander's office to report relative to an urgent matter. I reported and he informed me that my wife had filed for divorce. He told me that since I was on active duty, nothing could commence until I returned to the States. I was surprised but not shocked because I had been suspicious for quite a while since she had stopped answering my letters. I told my commander that I was not upset but rather relieved that it was out in the open. I was determined to serve out my remaining term of service and settle this problem when I returned home. I was discharged July 3, 1961.

Upon my return home, I called my ex-wife, since the divorce was final, and asked her to leave my car (1952 Ford sedan) at the curb in front of her house with the keys under the mat and I would pick it up the next morning. Brother George drove me over that day and I got my car back. Actually our marriage lasted only about 10 months if I deduct the military service time. I have not seen nor talked to her since.

The Chrysler Years

Following my military discharge I returned to my old job at Chrysler Defense Operations in August 1961. I was assigned to the design team working on a new all-aluminium cargo truck as well as special equipment options. During this period I was living at home with Sister Elizabeth, brothers Walter and Richard and

Mom & Dad. Sister Mary as I recall had gotten married and George was living alone at an apartment near Chrysler where he worked. I re-enrolled at Wayne State and continued my engineering studies.

Socially, I attended weekend single dances and events where I met new friends and acquaintances. At that time a popular event was singles' dances at the War Memorial Hall on Detroit's eastside. This is where I first met Florence. She attended these dances with several neighborhood friends. After the dance I would meet them at a local pizza parlor and visit. After a while Florence, Pinkie to her friends and family, we started casual dating. She was attending Detroit Business Institute (DBI) for a degree in the Secretarial field and I was attending night school at Wayne State. We dated steady for quite a while. She was Lutheran and attended church in St. Clair Shores, Michigan. We got along well and grew closer together.

Saturn Space Program - New Orleans

In early 1962 the Chrysler Missile Plant located in Warren, Michigan announced that they received a major contract to design the stage I booster rocket for the Saturn Program (1st moon launch). The design and engineering of the project was located in New Orleans with the design offices in the new Barrone Building, which was in the downtown retail area. The production of the Saturn rocket was at a suburban plant with close access to the Mississippi River. The plan was to float the Saturn rocket, when complete, down the Mississippi to the Gulf and then haul it to Cape Canaveral, Florida for the scheduled launch.

NASA's George C. Marshall Space Flight Center located in Huntsville, Alabama directed the Saturn project. This was the location that housed the World-War II, German scientists' team supervised by Ph.D. Wernher vonBraun, the renowned rocket and space expert. Von Braun and his team had surrendered to the U.S. Army offered their technical expertise to the U.S. government that relocated them and their families to the complex in Huntsville, Alabama.

Chrysler needed to staff the design work and solicited design engineers to transfer to New Orleans to work on the project. Still being single I volunteered and along with two other guys, Dave Gondoly & Tom Jacques and we headed for New Orleans in April 1962.

The three of us rented a two-bedroom apartment at an upscale apartment complex near Lake Ponchatrain. Most of the residents were younger people and with a large kidney-shaped pool it turned out to be party central. At first we all rode together to and from work at the new 20-story Barrone office building in downtown New Orleans. Due to various assignments, we ended-up with diverse schedules in different departments. After a short while we lost close contact on a daily basis and each of us commuted separately.

This office building was occupied by several aerospace companies. Among them were Martin-Marietta, Boeing, Rockwell, and Chrysler Space Division. Each of these companies was responsible for the design of their specific components for the Saturn rocket project. Each of these aerospace companies occupied separate floors in the Barrone Building.

New Orleans is not noted for an industrial/manufacturing economy and therefore there was a severe shortage of technical-skilled workers. It was common for the higher skilled employees to quit one of the suppliers and rehire at one of the others' as a promotion or better wage package. Therefore, many of the designers would come to work carrying a briefcase or box containing their drafting tools and instruments. Employee turnover was a major problem. I was transferred in with Chrysler and had seniority and automotive industry benefits.

My assignment was the thrust-structure that housed the articulating main rocket engine. This was the 1st stage rocket that lunched the entire two-stage missile and would eject (separate) at the threshold of the thinner outer space. The structure I worked on was fairly complex since it had to support the huge rocket as it articulated in multiple directions to maintain the trajectory path of the rocket and payload.

Two or three young detail draftsmen were also assigned to my project for supervision and training that also added to my workload. I was also responsible for the fabrication of the thrust-frame that supported the engine. This assignment required that I travel to and from the new rocket assembly plant several miles away by a shuttle service as the project progressed. At one particular meeting Werner vonBraun was in attendance and I had an opportunity to meet him personally.

During my visits to the assembly plant I met Woody, a friend of my sister Mary and we became buddies. Woody was the manager of the "clean-room" at the plant where all of the intricate electronic instruments were assembled and validated in a sterile environment. He had to dress in a white coverall and hood. For me it was an interesting experience to observe all of the various functions of the Saturn project.

Woody lived in the French Quarter (Vieux Carr'e) at the corner of Chartres & Esplanade in what was a slave-quarter apartment. Knowing that I was looking for another place to rent, he told me that the adjacent unit next to him was just vacated. I immediately went there, applied and was accepted by the owners'. This was a unique rental apartment complex. The construction of these units consisted of the owner's main brick house which faces the street and has a large wrought-iron gate opening to a corridor into a large patio surrounded by a series of two-story apartments that in the old-days housed the owner's slaves. There were six identical units. The layout consisted of a single room with a double-bed, a real fireplace, and toilet, sink and hand shower enclosure. The kitchen was similar to a boat galley with a small stove, refrigerator, and sink in the counter. It was closed-off by a louvered sliding wall-unit that opened to the entry door. All the units shared a long balcony over-looking a standing fountain on the patio.

During my time in New Orleans I also continued my education and attended evening classes at Tulane University and Louisiana State University (LSUNO).

Marriage to Florence (Pinkie)

Florence and I continued writing and phoning each other regularly. While I was working in New Orleans I had bought an engagement ring and on a short trip home I proposed marriage and we planned a church wedding for September 7, 1963. Following the wedding we drove to New Orleans where we lived in my little slave-quarter apartment.

New Orleans never sleeps and bars in the French Quarter stay open 24 hours, except for a city ordinance that requires ½ hour for clean-up maintenance. In the 'Quarter' at night there is continuous action, with sirens and loud jazz music. One block from our apartment there was a bar/restaurant named "Ruby Reds"; a Chicago style joint that served a famous ½ lb. burger and beer at all hours. With buckets of shelled peanuts on the bar, patrons would throw the shells on the floor. After a while, the floor was 6 inches deep to walk through; certainly the reason for a mandatory clean up.

Well, often when we were awoken we would we would get dressed and go to "Ruby Reds" for a burger in the middle-of-the-night. Another interesting thing about the 'Quarter' was the bus transportation to downtown. The main route was the "Desire Street" bus (that replaced the famous 'Street Car'). Only a mile long it made several stops and commuters would wait in 100 degree heat swatting swarms of mosquitoes with hanker-chiefs, hats or whatever until the bus arrived. It was a morning ordeal to get to work. Often we would cut-thru the air-conditioned department stores to get to the Barrone Building for work. Florence easily got a job at the Boeing Corporation and we worked in the same building but on different floors.

Occupying the 1st floor of the Barrone Building was the E.F. Hutton Brokerage Company. At lunch "time I would check the stock-market and ticker-tape that was housed in a large glass-dome for anyone to observe the latest stock-prices and news information. This habit of mine would put me in a position to witness a future historical event.

With both of us working we moved to a nicer apartment in Meterie, just outside of New Orleans. We made friends with an interesting couple in the complex. This couple from New York City were recently married and his father presented them with a business gift of a small chain of "Dairy Cream" restaurants to manage. They came from wealthy families and this gift was intended to advance their future. I remember that the bride was a daughter of the Hickey-Freeman family famous for the up-scale men's suits and clothing. We got along very well and shared entertainment events such as the "Mardi-Gras" and sightseeing. Florence's Mom and Dad did drive down for a visit to see our new apartment and spend time with us touring the New Orleans sights.

We often went to the "quarter" for the jazz music and leisure eating and the frequent jazz parades. A favorite place to listen to Dixieland music was the Preservation Hall where jazz legends played while patrons sat on the floor and offered donations for song requests. Pete Fountain's club on Bourbon Street was also a nice retreat. In the "quarter" you can carry your "Hurricane" drink on the street going from bar-to-bar for refills.

For our 1ˢᵗ Marti-Gras parade we dressed-out as matching "jail-birds" outfits and joined the continuous parade that seemed to last forever. The large noisy celebrating crowds wore every conceivable costume imaginable, and some very skimp or even none at all.

Another nice experience was a party trip on the "Delta Queen" paddle-boat that cruised the Mississippi complete with the sounds of the steam-whistles to treat on-lookers at the river bank. The festivities were sponsored by the Saturn program management as it was completing the design phase.

While in New Orleans I continued my education at night school. I first attended Tulane University in the city Garden District, taking the old-fashioned street-car to and from classes. The buildings and grounds surrounding Tulane are magnificent and represent what you would perceive the historic old-south to resemble. I also attended several classes at the LSU New Orleans campus on Lake Pontchartrain which is an extension of LSU known for its football fame. One of the classes I had to take was a required U.S. history course which was very interesting. The civil war history experience taught in the South differs in many respects relative to the political aftermath of how it is viewed elsewhere in the country. Actually, Wayne State University denied me transfer credit for the history course I completed at LSU.

On a Friday, November 22, 1963 I personally experienced a fateful event. It was lunchtime and I was at E.F. Hutton Brokerage watching the ticker-tape at E.F. Hutton, when at 12:30 the ticker-tape was spitting-out news (not numbers). There was an instant alarm, as I was reading aloud to the crowd that President Kennedy had been shot. People seated in the gallery came alive. There was pandemonium in the office and adjacent lobby. Surprisingly many of the people were cheering and happily excited. Being from the North it was very puzzling for me. This tragic event would play out over the next few weeks with businesses closed and work suspended for several days.

Return to Detroit

In early 1964, following Marti Gras, my work assignment was essentially complete and I received a transfer back to Chrysler's Engineering Center in Highland Park, Michigan in July 1964. I rented a small U-Haul trailer and Florence and I headed home to Detroit. Florence's Uncle Joe was a Great Lakes freighter Captain and was away on extended assignments and offered us his Westside Detroit apartment for several months. Following that, we rented a one-bedroom apartment in a brand new apartment complex in Warren, Michigan near the GM Tech Center. I was still working at Chrysler in Highland Park and Florence was hired at a General Electric Plant also in Warren. Her job was secretary/stenographer in the department that produced artificial diamonds used for industrial abrasives.

Since we only had one car, we bought a used car from one of Pinkie's workmates. It was a 1950's Peugeot and my first experience with a foreign car. This unusual car was a real learning experience. While it had been well maintained by the former owner, we experienced repair problems due to lack of and cost of replacement parts. Therefore, it was often out of service and not dependable.

My job at Chrysler Highland Park Engineering was designing car exhaust systems and bumpers. This was not a very interesting assignment, actually boring when compared to my former projects. To top it off I was seated at a very long drafting board that I had to share with another draftsman. In addition Chrysler technical employees were unionized and had to pay dues.

General Motors Fisher Body Division

In March 1965 I received a job offer at General Motors Fisher Body Division. This job was a real opportunity for me to expand my engineering experience into automotive design that would determine my future career.

My new job assignment was in the Research & Development Department. Fisher Body Division was the largest General Motors group and responsible for the design and manufacture of the automobile body for all domestic motor car divisions. This included Chevrolet, Pontiac, Buick, and Cadillac vehicles.

The auto body includes the vehicle exterior and interior structure, seating systems, interior trim, glass, carpet, paint and mechanisms, such as window regulators, door hinges, locks, seat adjusters, both manual & power regulated.

GM Brand Motor Divisions supply the drivable portion of the total vehicle. This includes the front-end sheet metal, engine and drive train, chassis-frame, engine and wheels.

The total vehicle (car) is the marriage of the body & drivable chassis. The vehicle is marketed by the specific GM Brand Motor Divisions through their individual dealerships to a wide range of potential buyers.

Our First Home

Now that I had a dependable job with a potential career, we decided it was time to move out of the rental apartment and into a home. We contracted with a builder in a new sub-division in Warren, Michigan close to the GM Technical Center. It took less than a year to build and we were anxious to move in. I remember having to lay sod to establish a lawn and hire a contractor to add a rear patio off our family room. Our new home was a nice all-brick, 3-bedroom single-story ranch-type house with a full-basement on a 60 foot lot on Bade Drive. This new subdivision was located just opposite the Macomb County Community College campus on 12 mile road.

Our son Stephen was born on August 26, 1967 and that was the start of our real family and the responsibility that came with it.

We lived at this Bade address for several years and during this period I received a promotion at GM Fisher Body that offered more challenging assignments and responsibility. I was very fortunate to have made this job change because the auto industry was to under-go fundamental design changes. The future focus would be to improve the safety of all its vehicles.

The Era of Auto Safety

In early 1965 the auto-industry came under severe scrutiny relative to automotive safety. Ralph Nader, a consumer advocate had published his famous book, "Unsafe at Any Speed"; that specifically addressed the 1960-1964 Chevrolet Corvair. The initial book criticism was related to the "controversial" swing-axle suspension that was subjective to the potential roll-over of the vehicle.

However, the entire automotive safety issues had become a public concern due to the increasing deaths and injuries in auto-accidents.

Prior to the "Ralph Nader" alert, there was very little emphasis on automotive interior safety. The result of this public safety awareness was the initiation of extensive research and design of all potential injury hazards that could injure vehicle occupants and especially children.

GM Fisher Body Division and in particular my department, "Product Research & Safety" (PR&S), was assigned to spearhead the research and design development for the interior safety for all GM passenger vehicles.

As my specific assignment I was charged with researching and identifying potential occupant injury hazards within the vehicle interior. The primary objective was to develop product design proposals to address the current safety issues that exist in the vehicle to achieve a friendlier interior.

This was related to any hazard that a seated occupant would be exposed to during an accidental crash. Obviously, seat belts would be required to protect an occupant against ejection out of his/her seated position and potentially out of the vehicle. A firmly seated person is restrained within a limited space. Therefore hazardous objects or surfaces in the head-impact area must be designed to be non-rigid and energy absorbing. My initial design proposals included soft crushable interior structure and energy-absorbing trim materials. This required static and dynamic testing to identify the human injury threshold that the component design would not exceed. These criteria became the goal for all future designs. The primary standard was developed by Professor Lawrence Patrick, Wayne State University. The Head Injury Criteria (HIC=1,000 or less) is still used today. Chest Acceleration of less than 80 m/sec is also a criterion.

Automotive Safety and Research

Safety issues are related to the many aspects of vehicle speed, handling and crashworthiness. Crashworthiness is a measure of survivability and reduction of potential injury of the vehicle occupants. This measurement has two-components.

The "first criteria" is the severity of the initial accident collision and the ability of the vehicle structure to absorb the crash energy and dissipate the acceleration forces to limit the potential harmful effects on the occupants. The actual crash is called the "First Collision" and the "second criteria" is the resulting reaction (deceleration) of the occupant and his/her potential impact into the vehicle interior structure/components. This is considered the "Second Collision".

The vehicle interior is designed to directly protect the occupants by maintaining the surrounding interior structure in what is called "the safety cage" that limits intrusion that could be hurtful to the occupants. The primary reason for using seatbelts is to contain the occupant within the vehicle and within the safety zone.

My assignments included the testing and analyses to achieve energy absorbing (EA) crush characteristics for occupant head impact into the instrument panel, windshield header and side pillars, sunshades, door structure, top-of-seat backs, armrests, etc. The primary design protocol provided collapsible components and support structure to achieve head deceleration levels that assured a safe human tolerance result.

Fortunately, GM Fisher Body had the foresight to have purchased and installed the 1st HYGE (Hydraulic-Controlled Gas-Energized) Impact Sled in the auto industry. This new tool allowed dynamic simulation of actual crash testing parameters. This equipment was installed in the Fisher Body test laboratory at the Milford, Michigan Proving Grounds. The lab was also equipped with the latest dynamic tools to test and evaluate the interior component energy-absorbing characteristics to ensure crashworthiness of the interior structure such as pillars, headers, doors, dashboard and potential injurious components.

An extensive test and design development was conducted at both the Fisher Body laboratories and at the GM Proving Grounds. I was assigned a Fisher Body bright yellow station-wagon (a canary) for my daily travel from the GM Technical Center in Warren to the Milford proving grounds. My two primary projects were the testing and development of energy-absorbing materials designed with special features and safety restraint systems.

The personal safety of vehicle occupants is dependent on their restraint system and its proper use. Seat design and seat belts are interrelated since they directly position the occupant and provide the primary safety-restraint within the vehicle. It was essential for us to determine the movement (kinematics) of a typical adult and or child under various crash conditions. To establish the criteria (data) it was necessary to dynamically test various-sized dummies that were both seat-belted and unbelted in different seated positions to generate reference data related to potential safety performance.

This basic research was developed using the Hyge sled testing at the GM Milford Proving Grounds. Important findings were used to establish several basic design principles for both the seat and the seat-belt position angles to ensure proper restraint. One basic criteria was the recline angle of the seat-cushion and its relationship to seatbelt (lap-belt) performance. This is referred to as the anti-submarining ramp. This seated ramp-angle inhibits a (smaller) occupant from sliding under the lap belt and assures maximum lower torso retention. This seat cushion development led the industry to what is known today as a "child booster seat." This design feature is present in all automotive seats and especially essential in child restraint systems and booster seats.

Our PR&S department was credited for the design of several unique safety features such as: (1) side door beams, (2) collapsible steering column, (3) laminated windshield glass, (4) skid header w/sunshade, (5) energy-absorbing instrument panel, (6) folding seat back locks and seat structural performance.

Also Fisher Body and the GM Ternstedt Division developed and introduced two child restraint systems that were marketed as "GM Love Seats". The 1st Child Safety Seat was introduced to the public at a U.S. Congressional Hearing on automobile safety in 1967. The 2nd unique child restraint system was the "rearward-facing" GM Infant Seat in 1970.

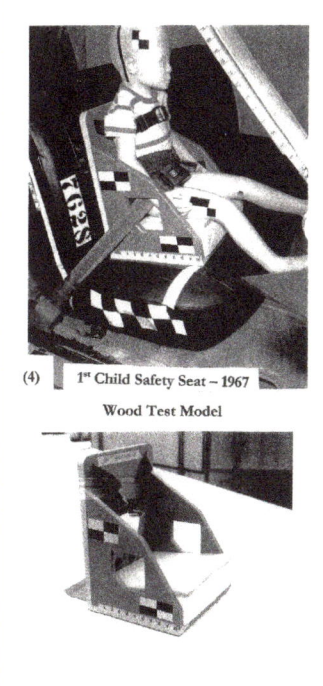

(4) 1st Child Safety Seat – 1967

Wood Test Model

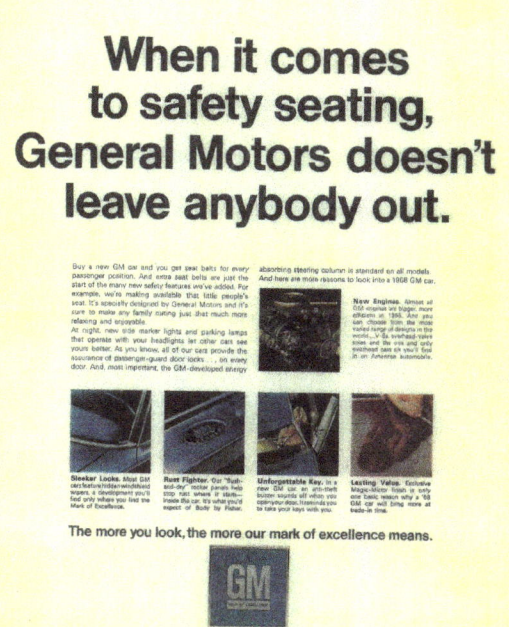

When it comes
to safety seating,
General Motors doesn't
leave anybody out.

The more you look, the more our mark of excellence means.

The 1st Child Safety Seat (GM Love Seat) - 1967

This was my signature project. This child restraint system (CRS) was designed for a child approximately 1 to 2 years-old seated in a forward-facing direction.

This 1st child safety seat was named "The GM Love Seat". As a child restraint system (CRS) it was dynamically tested on the Hyge sled and also barrier-crash-tested in a vehicle. The "GM Love Seat", was introduced as a dealership option in 1967 and was produced and sold by major retailers such as Sears, Montgomery Wards and several modified versions by juvenile products companies.

When I first started the child safety restraint project I was able to purchase many of the available child car seats on the market. These were the tubular-kind that typically hooked over the seat back (mostly passenger seat) that elevated the child for a better view. Some had an integral chest strap to hold the child. There were several varieties of these products. I tested all that were available on the Hyge sled and they proved to be a disaster; all were hazardous by design. The elevated child dummy flew thru the windshield opening, landing far down the sled-tracks. Initially Fisher Body management directed that we consider an optional child vest that would be secured using the vehicle lap belt. It turned-out to be impractical as well as hazardous. After continuous testing failures, I was very motivated to find a CRS solution.

I also had a personal reason to do so. My wife, Florence was pregnant with our 1st child at the time. Stephen was born August 26, 1967 and I was spurred to design a safe restraint system that would be practical; and especially safe for my son Steve.

Utilizing all of the knowledge I had gathered relative to dummy kinematics, seat belt loading and the anti-submarine cushion ramp, I designed a prototype child seat and constructed it out-of-mostly wood.

The wood structure was the platform (fixture) that provided for attachment of the components that configured the restraint system, but was not directly involved in the crash performance. Injection-molded structural plastic in an attractive configuration would replace the wood fixture in the final design. The anti-submarining ramp configuration would be molded into the plastic base structure. This is to maximize lap belt restraint and keep the child in a safe position to avoid forward excursion and head contact with the instrument panel. At that time, children were seated in either the front passenger seat or seated in a rear seating position.

The primary components of this first safety-tested CRS were:
1. The standard vehicle lap-belt used to secure both the child and the seat structure to the vehicle structure directly;
2. A "C"-shaped integral base plate would be inserted between the seat bottom and seat back bight-line to act as a torsional retainer, resisting forward rotation, of the child seat;
3. The seatbelt, when-tightened, envelops (encapsulates) the seat base structural gussets and the child's lower-torso to the vehicle's anchorage points;
4. A chest strap with a quick-release buckle secure the child's upper torso;
5. A rotating handrail (armrest) was provided as an option.

The wedge-shape cushion made of rigid foam was designed to maximize lap belt restraint and keep the child in a safe position to restrict forward excursion and head contact with the instrument panel or the front seatback for rear passengers.

In 1970 Fisher Body also introduced the 1st Rearward-Facing infant restraint system. This "GM Infant Love Seat" was also developed and tested on the Hyge sled as well as actual crash tests at the GM proving grounds. Today, all infants (under 2-years-old) are required (by law) to be seated rearward facing in the vehicle's rear seat.

Currently the quest for protecting children in all types of vehicles and varying seating positions has led to a proliferation of CRS models and types to accommodate all children from infants through early teens using a CRS or booster seat and vehicle seatbelt restraint combinations.

For example the CRS types, models and manufacturers has grown to 185 different models; manufactured by 28 independent companies.

This complexity has led NHTSA to introduce and rate the various CRS models by an annual "Ease of Use Rating" to assist the consumer in choosing the proper type of CRS for their specific child.

In future years I would publish two-books based on my experience in automotive safety and the early development and criteria for establishing safety standards and testing procedures. The original safety standards were issued by the U.S. Department of Commerce under the General Services Administration (GSA) for the purpose of imposing safety requirements for any company engaged in the sale of automotive vehicles to U.S. Government agencies. This was due to the public out-rage over the rising accidental deaths and serious injuries. The initial GSA standards were the fore-runner of what became the National Highway Transportation Safety Administration (NHTSA) and Federal Motor Vehicle Safety Standards (FMVSS).

My Safety Publications
1. "Don't be a Dummy!", A Primer on Automotive Safety: by- An Engineering Expert Witness. Pub. iUniverse, Inc. - ISBN# 978-1-4401-3556-9 (2009).
2. "Precious Cargo"- Promote Child Safety - iUniverse, Inc.-ISBN # 978-1-4620-1453-8 (2011).

At this time I continued attending Wayne State University in the evenings and finally graduated with a Bachelor of Science Degree in Mechanical Engineering in December 1970.

Shortly, after graduation I applied for, and passed a difficult exam to become registered as a Licensed Professional Engineer for the State of Michigan in October 1971. I passed the test and certification and was assigned PE # 18418. Michigan requires professional engineers to complete 30 hours of continuing education courses every 2-years for renewal of the license. The Professional Engineer designation was to become an essential requirement for my future career as an expert witness for legal litigation cases related to automotive safety. I would later form a company called Seat Consultants, LLC for this type of work.

Hatherly Village – Sterling Heights, MI

Kimberly Fay was born on June 5, 1970. Shortly afterwards, we decided to move to a larger house in a new up-scale subdivision in close-by Sterling Heights. This new home at 4534 Brockham Way in Hatherly Village was a 4-bedroom, 2-story colonial-style house. The 2nd floor was designed with 4-bedrooms and a large sitting room. We also had a nice large lot with a high landscaped grass berm facing a three-corner intersection with an open view. I also built a large wooden deck off of the family room into the fenced-in backyard.

Both Steve and Kim attended the new Hatherly Elementary School that was within walking distance. We regularly attended Faith Lutheran Church in Sterling Heights. I served on the Board of Trustees for a couple of years, responsible for budget projections, expenditures and building/property maintenance.

While we lived in Hatherly Village we had a very special experience. When the children were very young, I was introduced to Mr. Carlock, a sculptor, who had just finished a commission for a close neighbor. The neighbor engaged Mr. Carlock to complete a true-life head sculpture of his two young children. This artwork was very impressive and I felt that it would be very special to have full-head/chest sculpture of Steve & Kimberly that would be a family heirloom. Mr. Carlock was interested in doing this and quoted the time and cost.

Florence and I decided to have it done. Since we had a large upstairs family room, this became his studio. Kimberly and later Steve sat for long time periods while Carlock captured their profile and unique features. Florence still has these busts in her possession and hopefully one day Steve and Kim will share them with their children and friends.

While living in the Hatherly house we also had a terrible accidental experience. While mowing the back lawn using a manual reel mower, I stopped to empty the bag and the reel continued to spin. Kim, about 2 years old, wandered over to the lawn-mower and intrigued by the spinning blades, she stuck her finger into stop-it. Her finger was severed. Hearing the screaming, I rushed over and held her and the hanging finger back in-place. Florence and I wrapped her hand in a wet bloody-towel and rushed her to an emergency clinic close-by. They wrapped her hand & finger in ice and took her to the nearest hospital. A hand surgeon, Doctor Pouch, operated that evening and reattached this tiny-finger. I was a nightmare I will never forget. Thanks to Doctor Pouch and skilled the emergency personnel the operation was successful. I thanked the Lord for this medical miracle.

On a lighter side I remember telling Kim a bedtime story about a special little girl we named Sally Winkler. Sally had a lot of interesting friends. The idea behind the continuing tale was that girls can always out-do the boys. Without recounting the entire adventure odyssey, I remember many of the characters that I believe Kimberly would still remember?

Each of them provided the suspense and the climax of the issue we invented when we made-up the bedtime story. I recently ran across some notes (diary) that I recorded for a potential storybook. For the fun-of it, these are some of the leading cast of the "Sally Winkler Tales"

- Sally Winkler / her brother Johnny / dog Spot / skipping champion / Apple, her pony;
- Bruce the flagpole Bully / Bernadette the Judo/Karate champ / mailman & biting dog;
- Kersten Johnson / Sally's Mom & Dad;
- The major TV quiz / boys versus girls / Sally's school mates / and many other characters;
- Sun Lee Chic the math, computer, martial arts expert and her grandfather the ship designer.
  Some day in the future I may recreate these stories into a children's series of short stories to inspire and motivate youngsters.

During the period we lived in Sterling Heights I served as a Cub Scout Leader and acting Scoutmaster for Pack 198. I also was appointed and served as Commissioner or Board Chairman on the Building Board of Appeals, Housing Code and Fire Prevention Code for Sterling Heights for 6 years.

As a family we spent most of our spare time attending children's events, visiting friends and neighborhood activities. We did take a month-long vacation travelling across the country in our new Oldsmobile. We took the Southern route through the Rocky Mountains, Nevada and Southern California and Disney Land;

returning via the Northern Route. We had a good time and Florence had prepared special gifts to entertain Steve and Kim daily as we travelled.

I believe living in Hatherly Village as a young family was a pleasant and memorable experience for all of us.

Rochester, Michigan – 309 Grosse Pines Drive

In 1977 the Sterling Heights public teachers went on an extended strike. The school board and teachers union were at a stalemate and the threat that the schools would not reopen in the fall was almost certain. Both sides were very stubborn and distrustful of any potential settlement. We had been thinking about moving to a more desirable area like Rochester, Michigan where the latest housing and development was occurring. A favorite pastime of ours was viewing new model homes and locations so we were familiar with availability and pricing. We decided to have a house built in a new development called Grosse Pines in a prime Rochester location with future investment potential.

We Joined the St. John Lutheran Church and entered Kimberly in the St. John School for the fall term and Steve as a freshman at Lutheran High School North. During the house construction Florence drove the children back and forth from Sterling Heights to Rochester.

During the early years that we lived at 309 Grosse Pines Drive, we did a lot of family activities. I recall one Sunday afternoon sitting in our family room reading the newspaper when a major advertisement attracted my attention. It was fall and the Bavarian Village Sports store was running a special sale on all of their ski equipment. This included complete family ski- packages. We discussed the idea that maybe we should consider skiing as a hobby. I was not an avid skier but I had taken lessons thru the Detroit Free Press ski school. George and I had attended as beginners and liked the sport. Over the years I did ski with friends at the local ski areas and I thought we should try it as a family. Kim was 5 years old and Steve 8. Florence had never skied.

We decided to go to the store to get some idea of the cost and the likelihood that they could learn. Short story is that we bought skis, poles, boots and equipment for all of us.

At Thanksgiving time there was snow up in Boyne Country and that weekend we drove up to Petoskey and stayed at the Holiday Inn. The next morning we went to Boyne Mountain, unloaded our skis, poles and put-on our boots for the first-time. We bought tickets and headed for the beginners hill. It was a disaster. We couldn't get our skis-on, we slipped and fell-over and it was discouraging. I immediately walked to the ski-school office and hired two-instructors, one for Kim and the other for Steve & Florence. I told the instructors that I would pay for whatever it takes to get them going. It was worth it. In a few hours Kim was holding the tow rope with both hands over-her-head and snow-ploughing down. One instructor took-on Steve and actually put him on a chair lift to ski-down the beginner's hill. The other instructor worked with Kim and Florence and got them snow-ploughing down. I watched from aside and also practiced on the beginners' hill.

After our first day on the hill, we returned to the Holiday Inn, got in the hot-tub and had a great time. Everyone enjoyed the experience. Petoskey is a nice town and it was already decorated for Christmas making the trip a scenic winter-land. This became our annual vacation trip for several years.

Living in Rochester had great opportunities for weekend activities with close by cider mills, parks, craft shows, golf courses and ski-hills. Steve was actually a caddie for a while, and this also was an opportunity for him to learn the game and rules. Steve also took a liking to soccer and often practiced kicking and ball handling and he became very proficient.

Another interest of Steve's was joining the Rochester Karate/kickboxing club. We went to many of the class demonstrations; watching them break-boards with their hands and feet.

Rochester would become the home for the sport of Soccer. This world sport became a very popular in the U.S. for both adults and children. In the early 1970's there was a shortage of experienced engineers/designers for work in the auto-industry. As a result auto companies hired experienced designers on contract from the UK. These people were brought-over with temporary work-visas to fill these positions. Many settled in the Rochester area and they organized and coached the first soccer teams and games in the area. Rochester, Michigan became the leading location for soccer enthusiasts and Saturdays became famous for term "soccer-moms" who drove the children to the games and rooted for the young players. Steve and Kim would join the soccer rage and play every chance they could.

When the soccer leagues were first organized the little boys and girls were placed on the same team. This resulted in a big advantage for the boys.

Kimberly came home one afternoon after playing soccer. She was very upset and disappointed with her soccer team. Whenever Kim got a chance to score, the goalie would just grab the slow-moving ball and throw it back. She was a good athlete and a fast runner and this was very discouraging for her. When Kimberly was in grade school in Hatherly Village she was known for her quickness and able to out-run the boys during lunch break races for candy. She always won and the boys nicknamed her little "bluebird".

Well, to console her we made-up a bedtime story about ***a little girl, who became the best soccer player on an all-boys team.*** This was a night-to-night continuing chapter-to-chapter story. I would make-up this tale as we lay on her canopy-bed until she fell-asleep. The story would continue the next evening when I resumed the tale. This night time story was entitled "The Blue King". In later years (2003) I would embellish and complete this fanciful tale as a published children's storybook.

The published "Blue King" storybook will be covered in a later chapter since it became an obsession and legacy for me.

Graduate Education Continued

In 1979 I decided to continue my formal education and I applied for entry into a masters' program in Business Management at the Central Michigan Extension Campus in Troy, Michigan. This was a 2-year evenings/weekend course of study and I received a Master of Arts in December 1981.

Following graduation from Central Michigan, University, I received an invitation to consider entering a Doctorate program through Western Michigan University located in Kalamazoo, Michigan. However, this special program was being offered at the Selfridge Airbase in Harrison Township, Michigan. The airbase was considered part the WMU, Kalamazoo campus since the professors were being flown-in to teach the evening/weekend classes as part of the WMU flight training for pilot navigation over Lake St. Clair. I joined a group of well-qualified candidates living in the greater-Detroit area and military personnel assigned to service at Selfridge. The curriculum included the same course material as on WMU campus and required a final published dissertation. Some of the final courses had to be completed on campus by department professors and the dissertation defended in-person before the Graduate Academic Committee.

The title of my dissertation is: "The Relationship between Nonsupervisory Employees Self-Assessment of their Supervisory Skills and the Amount of Satisfaction they would receive from being a Supervisor".

The dissertation was based on a research study that I participated in as part of a General Motors Careers in Management training series offered to all eligible employees. One hundred fifteen non-supervisory salary employees participated in this program. The program consisted of 6 class sessions, with 2 & ½ hour-long evening meetings. I used the data that resulted from the management training seminars to support the conclusions arrived at in my dissertation.

My research method was based on the Sterling Institute's Career Development & Self-Assessment Guide. This survey guide documents how management candidates would perceive the role of becoming a supervisor and its duties and responsibilities. My dissertation was published in 1985 and is available to the public at the WMU Library. I graduated with a Doctor of Educational Leadership in August 1985.

Living in Rochester Continued

During the years in Rochester I continued working at GM-Fisher Body and on weekends I joined a group of fellow employees golfing on Saturday and sailing with Florence's brother Dennis and friends weekly in the evenings on Lake St. Clair. Their ship "Chesapeake" was a 50 ft. two-mast-schooner and we had some harrowing experiences. On one occasion we lost a sail and on another sailing date the engine caught-fire; the life-vests, stored in the engine compartment fell-onto the hot manifold due to rough-waves. We were able distinguish the fire and then limp back to the marina.

Florence, a stay-at-home mom, did engage in various hobbies such as pottery and art work. Later she would get involved in cultural dancing. We spent a lot of leisure time visiting her Brother Dennis, Nancy and family. They owned a unique cottage on "Stag Island", Canada located in the middle of the St. Clair River. The St Clair River borders both the U.S. and Canada. This small island is motor-less, no cars, and just one main sidewalk with most of the cottages facing Corunna, Canada. All of the cottages have boat docks reaching into the river. Access to the island was by a community ferry, from Corunna to the island. The ferry operates on-demand when a large signal-sign was raised & lowered from either side. Private boats could also dock at the island. Everyone knew one-another on this island and socialized together. A popular pastime was tubing-in-the river, as the current would deliver you to the other end. You would then walk back, carrying the big tube.

As a family we were also occupied with the activities of Steve and Kim. Steve played soccer & practised karate, Kim in gymnastics and both were engaged in separate school events.

Florence Enrolls at Oakland University

In the spring of 1982, with my encouragement, Florence decided to pursue her education and enrolled at nearby Oakland University. She signed-up for courses in dance and psychology which were her current interests. She met some new friends at the college that had similar interests and spent a lot of time with them. Steve and Kim were also attending their classes and returned home to what was often an empty house, waiting for their mom to come home.

Following the 1st semester Florence was attracted to an advertisement at Oakland University for a special study program at Oxford University in England. This one-month summer program (June-July 1982) would be fully credited toward her degree. She really wanted to do this, so I agreed to support her and we paid the tuition and expenses. Steve and Kim were mature enough to take care of everything while I was at work. Both of them had regular activities to keep them busy.

When Pinkie first got there we communicated regularly. However, for several weeks I did not hear from her. Finally when she returned home, I found out that she had met some friends at Oxford and they decided to skip the remaining classes and travel throughout England and Wales. When she returned she had bought me a Wales signature tie; bright green with the little red-dragon; as a gift. She was very pleased with the trip and we never discussed the fact that it was supposed to be a study course at Oxford. As far as I know she did not receive the credits from Oakland University.

The Russian Experience

After returning home from England, Pinkie re-enrolled at Oakland University for the 1982-83 winter Quarter. When she first returned to Oakland she met and joined in with a new group of liberal friends who spent their spare-time engaging in political events on campus. Soon after she became very independent and did not want to be responsible for any household chores. She came & left home as she pleased at various times and often returned late without any notice of her activities.

Early in 1983 Florence associated with a group of new friends that were members of a Ukrainian (Russian) dance group. This was a group of about twenty or so middle-age men and women she met through an Oakland University dance group. The dance group was scheduled to go on a goodwill tour to Russia and Romania. This event was sponsored by an Oakland University cultural organization. Florence joined this dance group and also wanted to take Kimberly along, because of her gymnastic skills. The trip was to last one month. However, prior to the goodwill tour, the dance group performed at local ethnic events and picnics as a fund-raiser. During this period Florence was seldom home and often returned very late or on occasion not at all. Florence would pay for the trip with money that was set aside for the children's education.

Kimberly was still attending St. John Grade School during the day and would return to an empty house and spent her time alone watching TV and waiting for me to come home from work. Since I was still working at GM-Fisher Body I wanted to make things easier for the children so I purchased a brand new 1984 Pontiac

Fiero sport-car on the GM Employee discount plan, for Steve. This made it possible for both Steve and Kim to attend their events.

In August 1983 Florence and Kim along with the Ukrainian dance group travelled to Russia for the one-month trip. During this time I did not have any contact with them.

Florence and Kim returned from Russia in September 1983. Florence went into seclusion, lighting candles all around the house, kneeling and saying continuous private prayers. I was puzzled and asked Kim what was going-on. She told me that her mom met a Russian man on the bus who was sad and needed help; she felt very sorry for him.

Periodically after she had returned home Florence received secretive phone calls and I was very curious. The next time a call came-in I over-heard it on an extension phone. It was from a Russian man (broken-English), I did not know his name, but he told her how much he was in love with his lovely Pinkie, and what she must do to bring him to America. He explains that she must go to the American Embassy and inform them that she was getting a divorce and she intends to marry her Russian boyfriend. She seeks travel permission for him to visit her. She apparently wrote down his directions and confesses her deep love for him.

I confronted her and she said that I have never been able to fill her needs and all she wants is to be left alone so she can enjoy her life. I find out she has been corresponding with him and she has re-enrolled at Oakland U. to study Russian history and language. I was concerned about this relationship and how it could affect Kimberly in the future.

Over the next few months Florence continued to communicate with the Russian. One day in late January 1984, I found an open letter from Russia addressed to Pinkie. I read the letter and I was surprised to find out the extent of the communication between her and the Russian over a period of time. He encouraged her to come and visit him.

They had exchanged phone calls and letters since she had returned from the trip to Russia. In addition she had sent him gifts, clothes and shared our personal and financial information. I found out that his name was Sergey (or something like that) when I read the letter. I could now account for many things that were missing from my wardrobe and closet. She also had been sending him valuable items that were mentioned in his letter and phone calls.

After reviewing the letter I contacted an ADAM lawyer (American Divorce Association for Men) that was recommended to me. My lawyer contacted the American Embassy to gain information relative to Americans traveling to the USSR. Relaying my experience they confirmed that the man on the bus was most likely a KGB agent. It was common for these trained agents to prey on American travellers, especially single women, to establish an on-going relationship. The objective was to get an invite to visit the U.S. and pursue a "green-card" or permanent status. They warned my attorney that this could put us in jeopardy and to be suspicious of future progress relative to his client. There is a history of Americans being detained in the USSR and subject to ransom.

In early March 1984 I received a phone call from Florence while I was at work asking if I could meet her for lunch at the Red Lobster restaurant near my work. I did meet her and she said the reason for the meeting was to inform me that she had hired an attorney and had filed for divorce.

That same afternoon I called and met with my attorney, explaining what transpired. He said that he was very familiar with the attorney she chose to hire. He told me that he was very familiar with her attorney, that she is very liberal, and a women's advocate. She will drag this thing out for all she can get.

He was aware of the Russian's influence and said I need to be very worried. He told me that since my wife just recently contacted her attorney, it is possible that the paperwork has not reached the court yet. He suggested that if I could file 1st, I would become the Plaintiff. This may protect Kimberly from becoming a pawn if Florence were to take her on a trip to Russia. I would lose any control if Florence is the plaintiff, as this is the case right now.

If I agree to file right now my attorney will draw-up the papers and go to the court when they open in the morning. If they had not yet filed, he will file for me immediately. I agreed and we drew-up the required papers and I signed them. Later the next day, my attorney called me at work to inform me that the court did not have any pending record of a divorce filing by her attorney. He then filed and I now became the plaintiff in this case. While it was favorable for me and protective of Kimberly, I would be criticized for initiating and causing the family break-up.

As a courtesy, I have redacted personal information regarding other matters that influenced our separation. The divorce was finalized on March 5, 1986.

<u>Tragedy Strikes Our Family</u>

October 17, 1985 was the saddest day of my life. My mother died of an adverse drug reaction. The hospital malfeasance was shocking. The doctor had prescribed a blood-thinner (Heparin), used to dissolve blood clots. His error was the dosage which exceeded the manufacturer's recommendation by three-times the safe limit. A 2nd doctor who was in residence at the time continued the dosage error.

Mom was initially admitted to a close-by hospital in Highland Park, at the outpatient clinic, affiliated with her health maintenance organization insurance plan.

Her physician at the clinic examined her. His initial diagnosis was a circulation problem in her left leg, probably due to a blood clot preventing the flow of blood to her foot, producing numbness. She was then admitted to the hospital for further analysis and treatment.

She was in exceptionally good health and this type of drug (Streptokinase) was commonly used to dissolve blood clots. Doctors knew that excessive bleeding was a potential concern and must be monitored. However, this warning was based on the recommended dosage; not on the excessive dosage that had mistakenly been prescribed.

Brother Richard, who holds a Doctor of Pharmacy degree and with many years of experience, was able to completely review all of the autopsy information. My Mom had suffered a terrible death. She went into "cardiac arrest". The autopsy showed that her liver had ruptured due to uncontrolled bleeding. Approximately 1-1/2 quarts of blood were found in the abdominal cavity. My mother had bled-to-death!

Brother Richard was so motivated by this dreadful experience that he spent the next few years researching the topic of the danger of hospitalization. In 1989 he published a learned pharmacy book in order to advise the public of what he had learned. This well researched book documents the ongoing problem of medication errors and adverse drug reactions that can occur in and out of hospitals. The public needs to be aware of this potential phenomenon and certainly discuss their concern with their doctor prior to his/her prescription. For further information refer to: ("Drug Death-A Danger of Hospitalization", Richard P. Hoffmann, Pharm.D., Pub. Charles C. Thomas, 1989, ISBN-0-398-0554-80).

The Tragedy Continues – My Dad Dies, One Year Later

Dad was very distraught and lost all interest in life at the loss of his wife of 53 years. He stopped socializing and lost his appetite, leading to a 70-pound weight loss. Exactly one year after our mother's death, Dad was admitted to the intensive care unit at another hospital, where he died six weeks later.

My sister Mary developed what we believe to be stress-induced hyperthyroidism and other family members remain distraught and anguished over the loss of our parents due to a situation that we believe was entirely preventable.

My GM Career Continues

Following my last divorce and the tragic death of my parents I was determined to concentrate my life and career on achieving at the highest potential my engineering experience and education would allow.

I continued my job at GM-Fisher Body as an engineering group manager in charge of advanced research projects and the production release of engineering specifications for special products.

This was a period of time when the U.S. auto industry was being challenged by increasing foreign import sales. GM in particular was suffering declining sales, as their larger gas-consuming vehicle models were losing in popularity.

The General Motors Reorganization

In 1984 General Motors was undergoing an introspective challenge as how to address foreign competition. The Japanese car-makers were eroding the domestic market. Competition was intense and all of the GM product lines were suffering due to lack of distinctive model offerings. McKinsey & Company, a premier worldwide management consulting group was retained by GM to research all sources of the automobile business including the design, management, organization and consumers to determine the cause of declining sales. Knowledgeable McKinsey consultants conducted in depth interviews with potential customers, GM managers, design engineers and industry observers to identify the critical issues. The motor car divisions, Chevrolet, Pontiac, Oldsmobile, Buick and Cadillac identified the Fisher Body Division as the focus of their main problems. These issues were the non-distinctive styling and common features that restricted their individuality.

Fisher Body Division was by far the largest and most profitable GM enterprise. Fisher Body was responsible for the engineering, design and manufacture of the complete vehicle body and components. This included glass, interior trim, carpet, paint, door hardware (locks, hinges, operating- mechanisms), seat systems and interior safety performance. The exterior sheet metal however defined GM vehicles and the various models looked very similar and were not distinguished between the car divisions.

Standardization of all these components among the various car body-platforms had been the key to GM's former success and profitability. Car body-platforms were designated as "A, B, C, H, X, E & K" and shared among all of the Motor Car Divisions. Certain DNA features were restricted to minimal differences to reduce proliferation of components and assembly requirements.

Dissolution of Fisher Body Division

Based upon the McKinsey research, GM ordered the dissolution of the Fisher Body Division and the redistribution of the various responsibilities among the Motor Car Groups and the consolidation of the major interior elements such as hardware and trim into new groups called Inland-Fisher-Guide Group (IFG) and the Delphi Group.

As a senior engineering group manager, familiar with all aspects of the previous Fisher Body operations and safety implications, I was assigned as Chairman of the Fisher Body Reorganization team. As chairman it was my responsibility to decide, organize and reassign all employee and design assets to accomplish the greater reorganization of GM into (1) Buick-Oldsmobile-Cadillac, BOC, or the large-car group and (2) Chevrolet-Pontiac-GM-Canada, CPC, or small-car group. This proved to be a monumental task with 10-12 hour days and much consternation because many fellow-employees were worried about their personal disposition. The final outcome was a successful transition for all concerned employees and management.

Ferris State Training Program

I was personally assigned to the new Inland-Fisher-Guide Division (IFG). My job was Engineering Group Manager for design specifications and advanced research projects.

As a new GM group we were allowed approx. 50-60 open-requisitions to hire new employees to fill essential positions. The engineering director of IFG and personnel manager asked me to establish a training program for these new employees. We had a relationship with Ferris State University in Big Rapids, Michigan and engaged them to support an off-site GM-IFG employee-training program. We organized an accelerated-training program to teach newly hired IFG employees, GM design and operating procedures, which comply with the corporate design and release requirements as well as cultural expectations.

This new-employee training program was organized and scheduled on a rotating one-week small group sessions on the Ferris State campus. Approximately 60 new employees attended these training sessions. Students were accommodated in a block of 1 & 2 bedroom condos on campus that were normally used for Ferris State board & visiting professors. I was also appointed to the Ferris State Engineering Advisory Board. This new GM training program was later adopted by other GM affiliates for their new employee training programs.

The GM-IFG Buy-Out

Due to the GM reorganization and the dissolution of Fisher Body Division I felt that my potential future advancement at GM was limited and GM itself could be facing bankruptcy. Many older, more senior employees were being offered a lump-sum buy-out. I was told that I could request to be included. I was deeply in-debt because of the divorce so the buy-out was offered and I accepted. I continued working at GM-IFG until April 30, 1988 when the buy-out was completed.

After leaving GM-IFG, I was hired on-contract by Modern Engineering and assigned as the program manager at the GM Seat Design Project Center in Warren, Michigan. The project we were working on was scheduled for the new E/K Cadillac/Buick/Olds luxury models and included several advanced engineering features such as 8-way power front seat adjustment with heated/cooled seat options. As that program entered production I was laid-off and had to seek another job.

Ruecker Engineering Ltd., a German contract engineering company operating in the U.S., offered me a position as Sales Manager for their extended business pursuits. This was a salary plus commission job that proved to be somewhat lucrative and included a company car. Many of the designers at Ruecker were recent Fisher Body retirees. This gave me a network of supplier companies that would trust Ruecker with new engineering contracts. Everything went well for the first year, but then Ruecker discontinued my base salary and reduced my commission agreement to save money. They kept their new work contracts I had established for themselves. I left that job and thought about starting my own unique firm.

The Education of Stephen and Kimberly

Both Steve and Kim attended and graduated from Lutheran High School North. This private parochial high school has a high academic reputation so that entrance exams for college entry are not required at most colleges. They were both accepted by colleges of their choice immediately following graduation from Lutheran High School North.

Stephen – Alma College & Internship Experiences

Stephen attended Alma College in Michigan and studied International Business. During his senior year he was selected to attend an internship in Germany. His language major was German so this gave him an opportunity to customize his pronunciation and reflect the local accent. He stayed in the household of a German family living like the typical German student. This included all reading, writing and studying in German and experiencing the local culture.

Following the college study program he returned home and soon thereafter he was offered a summer internship position by Ruecker Engineering to work in Germany at their Frankfurt office. Steve was very proficient in German and he had studied international business. Steve, however did not know how to drive a stick shift vehicle and that would be required all-over Europe. Part of my job was overseeing the GM-IFG engineering car fleet that was used to evaluate experimental design proposals. We had a new Pontiac Firebird (with a standard transmission) available and I checked it out for the weekend. Steve and I spent the whole-weekend teaching and practicing driving the stick shift. Steve then spent the summer at this job and became familiar with the various cultural regions of the country since he delivered drawings and parts to the several Ruecker offices in Germany.

During his stay in Germany I had an opportunity to visit him and do some traveling. GM-IFG had a design office in Russelsheim, serving GM-Opel and I had a temporary assignment there. When I arrived, Steve picked me up at the Frankfurt airport driving a small-pickup truck belonging to Ruecker Engineering. He drove me to a hotel in Wiesbaden where the GM people typically stay. I could not believe the road-trip. Steve was driving that truck like a race car; maneuvering thru the villages, up-shifting / down-shifting on the narrow hilly-streets and trusting on the blind-corner mirrors mounted on the small buildings. It was a very scary trip. Especially since I knew he had just recently learned to drive a four-speed.

While I was in Germany we decided to visit relatives in West Berlin. This involved driving thru Check-Point Charlie into the Communist East Berlin corridor. Entering East Berlin the guards pulled-us out of the car and quickly searched us and the car. We were then routed thru the Russian army camp in a stop & go fashion as armed troops crossed in front of us with a tank or truck parked at the corners. It was meant to be intimidating. Driving thru the high-way corridor was also a spooky trip to get to West Berlin. Camouflaged police cars would enter from off-road and follow-us and then disappear again. We had to find a toilet, so we stopped at a roadside restaurant. As soon as we entered, the place went totally silent. Everyone stared at us as we found the men's room. No one spoke nor did they point the way to the toilet. We finished and left. We did visit our relatives, gave them the cigarettes and chocolate we had brought and kept hidden in the car; returning the same day.

Another memory I want to share involves Steve and his accident experience. Steve was visiting a classmate friend and family. They lived in a house on a small hill and he had left the Ruecker truck he was driving in the driveway. He either forgot or did not secure the parking brakes. While he was inside the house the truck rolled downward, crossed the street and crashed into the fence, shrubs and porch of the neighbor's house below. There was a loud commotion and the police arrived. In Germany we found-out that very few people have insurance. The responsible party settles disputes in cash. The procedure is that an accident investigator reviews the damage and assesses the house, fence, landscaping and vehicles individually and bills the responsible party. Because Ruecker Engineering owned the truck they were assessed and had to pay the damages of about $5,000 U.S.

I received a call at work in the U.S. with this information and a demand for reimbursement to Ruecker. I didn't have that amount of money so we had to negotiate a longer-term work contract for them to recover their expenses.

At the end of the summer job Steve returned home. A GM-IFG Chief-Engineer had an opening for a department administrator and Stephen got the job as a full-time GM employee. Since Steve now had a good job, I bought a nice condo for him that was for sale in the Riviera Estates in the same complex that my Brother George lived.

Kimberly- Albion College & Wayne State Law School

Kimberly attended Albion College, Michigan majoring in pre-law. I remember driving back and forth with her delivering her belongings until she got settled. Once joining a sorority she moved into the clubhouse with her new friends. At that time we bought her a little Chevrolet Chevette, that she named "Jake". I visited her regularly and we attended a number of Daddy-Daughter activities.

Upon graduation from Albion College, Kim enrolled at Wayne State Law School where she graduated as an attorney and worked for a local Detroit Law firm. One of her assignments involved the litigation issue of the Ford Motor Company relative to the horrific Pinto fire defect case.

Kim's specialty was in contract law and she was hired as an attorney negotiating contracts for the placement of equipment and facilities for the relatively new cell-phone industry. She would later-in-life return to this wireless industry that is very competitive. I believe she has a great future due to her wide-range of experience.

In later years Kimberly and Robert Bloink were married and I would gain my first granddaughter, Abigail Faye Bloink on April 5, 2005.

<u>400 On the Lake – Harrison Township. MI.</u>

Following the GM buyout I continued to look for a permanent home that would accommodate both Steve and me. I was deeply in-debt and my credit rating destroyed. I was told about an unfinished condominium unit that was available in a 42 unit high-rise complex on Lake St Clair where several other GM managers lived. This was the last unit for sale. It had an obstructed view of the lake and the interior was unfinished, except for the dividing walls. The complex had a marina, clubhouse, pool and lower-level inside parking garages. It was called "400 on-the Lake" in Harrison Township. It was priced for a quick sale and once finished it would be a great investment.

I discussed the potential of buying this unit, with my banker, but my credit rating was very bad and I was turned down by another credit union. The good news was in my family, Brother Richard offered to buy it for me, in his name and in the future I would reimburse him and have the condo re-titled. We completed the sale and I now had a place to live.

This condo-unit however, was not move-in ready since it was basically a shell, without the finish plumbing, electrical or kitchen appliances. Nick Kuzdak a good friend of mine was a purchasing manager for the Chevrolet Division and he had great contacts with all-types of component suppliers and his daughter was just hired into my group at GM-IFG. Within a month or so my condo was painted, carpeted and essential plumbing and cabinetry installed. We had two-bedrooms, two-baths, family room and full-kitchen. Steve and I moved in shortly afterward. I did owe a number of favors to a lot of people and I did repay in full over time.

The GM-IFG buy-out settlement allowed me to re-establish my credit rating and to re-title the 400-on-the-Lake condominium I was now living in at a later date.

Steve did not live with me very long because he enrolled at Alma College and lived in the dorm. Later he would complete an internship in Germany and return home.

After a while Kimberly and her Mom were not getting along well and Kim asked if she could live with me in the condo. Of course I said yes. The first thing we did was to buy her a brand new bedroom suite at Sweden House. She was to live with me until she enrolled at Albion College and joined the sorority living at their private house.

Living at the condo on Lake St. Clair allowed me to return to a normal lifestyle and social contacts. One of the first things I did was to buy a power boat since I had a designated boat-slip in the condo marina. I bought the 26 foot, 1982 SeaRay-Sundancer from a retiring Fisher Body friend who had kept this boat in immaculate condition. I never had a boat before and my experienced buddies Tom Blake & Mark Dale offered to teach me how to handle-it. It was a single-engine outboard that required some tricky maneuvering to dock-it, especially in tight places. We had a great time out on the boat as I learned how to handle it.

A traditional summer event was the "jobbie-nooners" weekend at Gull Island in Lake St. Clair. This event was organized by a group of contract employees in the auto-supplier chain to celebrate their job status. On the Friday prior to that weekend, many of the job-shop guys would quit-work early before noon and head-out to Gull Island. Hundreds participated in what became a wild unending party. The topless volleyball competition was especially popular. It was understood that silence be observed until late Sunday morning for the sleep-ins.

Other events such as ice fishing and cross-country skiing on the lake were also popular. With numerous ice-shanties and pop-up tents scattered over the lake, I would leisurely ski-walk out to the various fishermen hunkered-down over their circular-cut holes hoping for a bite. They all had a brown-bag with schnapps' bottle and they would offer you a drink. They would always ask where the fish were biting and then sometimes they would pick-up and move. Some of the shanties were actually heated and had a portable TV. It was always a friendly environment and enjoyable experience.

Many homes on the lake would clear spaces for an ice-skating rink and that was also a good sport as well as hockey. I did do some skating and I still had my Canadian Flyer racing skates from my youth. In those days we went skating on "Belle Isle". I did compete in the "Gold & Silver" skate races, but I was only an amateur skater.

Looking-back when Kim lived with me at the condo, we went on vacation to Vail, Colorado skiing. Just Kim and I and we stayed at the Holiday Inn at Vail with all of the amenities including the hot-tub and pool after skiing. This was a memorable trip and we had a fun-time together.

Career Change - Becoming an Entrepreneur

Based on my design & engineering experience I believed there was an opportunity to organize a business offering unique engineering and design services that were not generally available by U.S. domestic contract companies. At Fisher body and later GM-IFG I was responsible for managing engineering contract help and aware that there was a severe shortage of qualified and experienced automotive engineers and designers in the U.S. However, in the United Kingdom, auto designers, were required to serve a 2-year apprenticeship to qualify to work in the UK auto industry. These apprenticeships were offered by Ford, Vauxhall, Bentley, Jaguar, etc. Several foreign contract companies were placing these qualified, experienced designers for short-term critical assignments in the U.S. using the temporary visa process.

I was considering a new-type of contract engineering company and staffing it with graduate-level engineers from Eastern Europe to work in the U.S. using the temporary H-2 visa process. We would then train these candidates in the use of computer-aided-design (CAD).

Currently CAD systems are basically being used as a digital drafting tool that replaced the manual drawing board technique. Former board-designers develop the component parts and assembly based on need, function and requirements. A prototype is then built for testing and review. Engineering calculations and analysis is not typically done by a designer, however, sophisticated CAD systems can be utilized to completely engineer the product.

To obtain a work visa these European engineers would be required to have a Masters or Doctorate Degree therefore they were very qualified to do advanced engineering, stress analysis, and simulated computerized testing of critical components.

Going forward, I discussed this idea with my business contacts, managers and close retiree friends and there was agreement that a contract engineering company offering these advanced skills would be successful. I recruited two-partners and we invested $5,000 each to start the process.

TEAM Resources Corporation

In 1989 TEAM Resources, Inc. was incorporated. (TEAM is an acronym for Technical, Engineering, Administrative and Management Resources). I was elected as President, Jim Morris as Director of operations, and John Langmesser as Secretary. My son Steve would also become a partner of TEAM as our business manager, handling all of the accounting and financial requirements. As a corporation we could offer a wide range of design and engineering and prototype build experience utilizing our many industry contacts.

In the beginning we introduced TEAM Resources Inc., to potential clients and shortly thereafter we were awarded a one-year contract by Inland Fisher Guide. We had 6 full-time employees plus we also were working on site at IFG. Two of our employees were Romanian engineers and Dr. Artur Dlugosz was a Polish Professor and mechanisms expert from the University of Warsaw, Poland.

My partner, Jim Morris had a close relationship with the Romanian community in Detroit. As a result we organized a recruitment team in Eastern Europe where highly skilled engineers were available. We engaged an immigration attorney who was able to obtained work visas for the foreign engineers and hired them on-contract with TEAM.

In order to train these workers in U.S. design procedures and processes as well as computer-aided design we registered our school as "TEAM Academy of Mechanical Design" with the State of Michigan. TEAM Academy contracted with Marisa Engineering Inc., to provide 'Catia' computer aided design (CAD) work stations and support for training these European engineers in advanced engineering applications using CAD.

Team Resources, Inc. became a diversified contract engineering firm. We placed engineers at several large automotive supplier companies as well as on-site design of advanced seating and safety systems. One of our job contracts involved a significant assignment through GM Legal Staff that would have future consequences for my career. Over time TEAM expanded to include as many as 60 employees.

TEAM Resources, Inc. was successful going forward. Our customer base included many tier-one automotive supplier companies. Especially companies engaged in automotive interior systems such as seating systems, interior trim, mechanisms (locks, hinges, adjustment hardware, safety systems and electronics). Tier-one suppliers design manufacture, deliver complete interior systems directly to Ford, GM, Chrysler, and foreign auto-makers. Our primary customers were Johnson Controls (JCI), Lear Corp, Faurecia and GM Delphi. JCI also had a branch in Burschied, Germany were we also employed contract staff. I also was on contract at JCI as a program manager and spent time in Germany.

While working inside our customers' facilities on new design projects we were issued several patents for new idea components. These inventions became the propriety property of the customer and this enhanced our engineering reputation. Hank Bucciero, a longtime associate, became our customer representative for outside prototype shops. Hank was a mechanical spring expert and inventor. This affiliation brought-in commission receipts for contract sales of our own technology patents.

One of these patents involved Beaver Tubing Company that developed our idea of replacing welded-on linkage-arms on power seat adjuster torsion-tubes with a unique-crimping operation. This was a major cost and quality savings for JCI. This tube-crimping operation resembles the type of fastening used to secure stepping-rungs on aluminum extension-ladders.

Working with Beaver Tubing Company; TEAM expanded our business scope to include representing other supplier companies. To enhance our image and contact base we became members of the Detroit Athletic Club. The DAC membership included legal, business and manufacturers that share common interests. Our DAC membership provided TEAM the ability to schedule business luncheon meetings, customer entertainment and expanding business opportunities. We have sponsored a number of events and have many memorable experiences.

TEAM and the GM Legal Staff Project

As the chairman of the Fisher Body Reorganization I was contacted by the GM Legal Staff to investigate an ongoing problem. GM was experiencing a severe problem in providing the documentation required for meeting court-ordered "discovery" information for their many product litigation cases. Actually, in certain cases the document delay to the court and litigants resulted in daily fine assessments against GM and that could also influence the litigation outcome.

The basic problem was a result of the GM reorganization and collateral effects. When Fisher Body Division was dissolved, the entire safety testing document retention center, housed at the GM Proving Grounds Fisher Body facility was dismantled and moved to the then vacant Argonaut Building at the GM New Center in Detroit. This historical testing and safety validation documentation contained film, videos, test reports, photos, and FMVSS documents related to all of the GM vehicles' history.

These critical files were delivered by a commercial trucking company and were contained in various metal file cabinets, boxes and cassettes. These files were numbered and contained the complete testing and validation history of the design of each particular vehicle. One whole floor of the Argonaut Building was dedicated for this purpose. A Detroit new center law firm was the custodian of this information and their law clerks were unfamiliar with the filing system.

As new litigation cases proceeded into the discovery phase, these files were accessed by various legal assistants in order to respond to discovery requests by the plaintiffs'. In the process the files were reorganized and re-filed using general categories such as testing, car models, videos, and FMVSS documents. Over time the information in the files lost the continuity to the specific vehicles under litigation and the original files could not be re-assembled. It was a horrendous situation.

I was very familiar with all of this safety documentation and engineering-design specifications. I toured the 4th floor of the Argonaut building and surveyed and assessed the damage. I estimated it would take a group of about 10 experienced engineering specification people to do the job of reassembling the files about 6 months. TEAM Resources was retained by GM Legal Staff to do this work. GM assigned a senior vice-president to oversee this confidential project and report progress on a weekly schedule.

Fortunately, for us, GM had recently offered buy-outs to many employees and this included a number of qualified engineering specifications people. TEAM hired about 10 of these retirees and we were allowed to occupy the entire 3rd floor of the Argonaut Building for the project.

There was an interesting sideline to this. We were allowed to park in the underground New Center parking garage, with access to the under-street tunnel directly to the Argonaut Building with an elevator to our floor. Upon arriving to work each day we were referred to as the "silver techs" by the legal staff people. We worked very diligently for the next 6 months reorganizing the safety documentation. As we proceeded GM hired Electronic Data Systems (EDS) (Ross Perot's company) to scan and digitize all of the legal information into an accessible data base.

Because I now had knowledge of all of the available documentation and legal discovery packages I was asked to represent GM as their Corporate Expert Witness in a number of on-going litigation cases.

As part of my assignment working at GM Legal Staff I also directed a special project to establish the GM Seat Design Information Center. This central document archive was housed at a law firm in Washington, DC and was available for all litigants involved in accident cases related to rear-impact, automotive seat and occupant safety issues for a nominal fee.

TEAM Resources Events and Special Occasions

TEAM was an employee-centered company and as such we sponsored numerous events for our employees and customers. All employees were eligible for full benefits, including health-care, 401 K donations, vacation and holiday pay as well as free CAD training.

TEAM also joined several social organizations, such as The Skyline Club, Detroit Athletic Club and The Renaissance Club. On special occasions we sponsored dinner parties, as well as participated in customer golf tournaments.

The TEAM annual picnic at Metropolitan Park was an outstanding event. Carolyn Hoffmann organized this picnic and participants. She hired a professional clown for the kids. We also had a portrait artist that did cartoon characterizations of people as friendly keepsakes. Carolyn hired a real butcher who furnished the meat and did the cooking to your personal choice or request.

An outstanding event was the money scramble for children. We bought several large buckets and filled them with 50 lbs. bags of birdseed. We donated $200.00 dollars of the various silver coins, including some silver dollars and spilled them into the buckets. Children, by age, were given a few minutes to fish for the coins to put into their little buckets. Some of the little kids thought they were rich. The older kids did a similar scramble on the grass filled with piles of birdseed & silver coins.

Another annual event was the soccer game among the employees and guests. This was a very interesting event since many of the employees were from the UK and/or European countries. The competition was intense but very friendly. We considered the game like a perk with the players looking forward to it as part of the picnic agenda.

TEAM Resources, Inc. - Tribute

Over time TEAM expanded to include as many as 60 employees. In 1994, TEAM Resources, Inc. received a Special Tribute for outstanding accomplishments as one of the "Future 50 Companies of Greater

Detroit". We went on to receive this honor for three consecutive years (1994, 1995 & 1996). In 1996 we received a commendation letter from Governor John Engler of Michigan for being one of the 100 fastest growing private companies in Michigan.

The Twin-Tower tragedy of 911, 2001 was to have a profound effect on TEAM. New temporary work visas and renewals were halted. The net result was that all current visa employees were directly hired as employees of our customer companies. TEAM continued in business but as a much smaller firm. It is still currently active as an engineering, patent and legal consulting company.

Seat Consultants, LLC

Following our TEAM assignments at GM Legal I was asked to separate any of the legal consulting projects I was involved with to distinguish between my personal work and any work related to GM. Currently I continue to act as a consultant and expert witness for law firms and companies representing both the Plaintiff and/or Defendant.

I believe that my involvement in several of these cases was very instrumental in resolving disputes that resulted in alleviating the remorse and financial obligations of the plaintiff and/or family that was injured or lost due to the unfortunate accident.

My expertise is in litigation or product recall cases involving child restraint systems (CRS) and rear-impact collisions. I am typically retained as a consultant and/or expert witness.

Since I am familiar with CRS and automotive seat design and manufacture, I continue to follow the latest product designs for my personal evaluation.

As a public service, I have on occasion contacted the National Highway Transportation Safety Administration (NHTSA) or the Consumer Product Safety Commission (CPSC) in order to notify them of potential safety hazards that believe could be harmful and may require investigation.

The Story Continues

With the establishment of TEAM Resources, Inc., I was independent and self-sufficient. This allowed me to pursue my position as an entrepreneur for business activities but more important was to reestablish a personal and social life. I had gone through several trying experiences and I just wanted to lead a normal lifestyle without focusing on the past.

Steve and Kimberly were now independent and I only wanted to maintain a loving and caring relationship. I would always be there for them if necessary but I wanted them to do whatever they wanted to pursue.

I now lived alone at my lakeside condo and free to do whatever I chose. I had made quite a few friends and we did things that were in our common interest. Many activities were business related and some were social. A few were former classmates and friends-of-friends. I frequently joined other GM people and supplier associates after work for drinks and conversation. I was not lonely and I had many interests.

One of these activities was to attend the Friday night singles dances at the various hotels or community convention halls. The most popular singles events were at the Troy-Hilton and the BBT (Birmingham, Bloomfield, and Troy) dances at the Kingsley Inn in Bloomfield Hills. Over time I had met and casually dated several gals and enjoyed those experiences.

On one of these occasions I met a special lady that would become my friend, a TEAM employee and eventually my wife. This particular singles dance was at the Kingsley Inn and Carolyn was there with her girlfriend, Sherri. I danced with both of them, but I favored Carolyn. We talked a while, exchanging pleasantries. She asked about my job and where I worked.

I had recently quit GM-IFG with the buy-out and I was working on contract with Modern Engineering. She was very surprised because it was a real coincidence that both she and Sherri also worked at Modern Engineering, in the Personnel Department. During our conversation she asked my age and I told her I was 50.

I didn't see her again until the next singles dance and we were both surprised. Carolyn and Sherri (breaking all the rules of personnel discretion) accessed my personal file at Modern Engineering and found-out that I had lied about my age. I was 53 and not 50! I told her it was not a lie; it was my approximate age and not a crime. Our conversation was cordial, but it was a little embarrassing. She did apologize for the violation of my privacy file and all was forgiven. During our conversation I found out that her hobby was dog-showing. She owned 2 Bearded Collie sheep dogs and was training them for a coming event. Actually, Carolyn had sold a dog to Sherri, so they had a lot in common.

Carolyn lived in Walled Lake but worked in Warren, so she often stayed with her twin-sister Marilyn who lived in Madison Heights with husband Louis and son Kurt. Louis and Marilyn lived in a unique subdivision that was patterned after and resembled what a Frank Lloyd Wright village might look like. It was a relatively small housing development with homes resembling Frank Lloyd Wright architecture. The houses did not have basements and were built over a crawlspace. This development did not have city water and a well-system and septic-system served the residents. The streets were asphalt with drainage-ditch shoulders.

I asked her out for our 1st date and to show her my condo. I guess she was leery and gave Marilyn my contact info as precaution in case she wasn't home at a reasonable time or not at all. Well everything went very well and I proved to be a perfect gentleman.

In the future I would drive the long excursion to her place in Walled Lake. Carolyn lived in a unique setting. She had an upstairs-apartment over her Dad's former garage-workshop. Her Dad (Elmer) was retired from his plumbing business and the workshop was mostly storage now. Carolyn lived with her dogs in this small apartment. The family property of 18 acres contained their ranch home, the garage-shop and another 2-story home belonging to her Aunt and Uncle. All of these buildings were separated and the property bordered a golf course. The Conrad family consisted of Dad Elmer, Mother Geraldine, twins, Marilyn & Carolyn and two married brothers Daniel and David.

We started to date steady and I was accepted by her family and included in holiday dinners. Carolyn continued working at Modern Engineering and I worked nearby at an office near the GM Tech Center.

When we first started dating steady I would often pick-up lunch for us and meet at Marilyn's house, where she would let the doggies out.

Not very long after we met, Louis and Marilyn bought a house that was for sale just across the street from them in the Madison Heights subdivision. They offered to rent it to Carolyn. This was a great move for her. The house required quite a bit of renovation and Louis contracted for a new kitchen and cabinetry. I helped Carolyn renovate and paint the living area and fireplace. It turned out to be very quaint and livable. The best part of this house was the large-size lot. It was all fenced-in that was great for the dogs. Also it had a large in-ground pool. I should also add that it had a lot of grass to cut and a wrap-around hedge that I ended-up cutting.

I continued living at my condo and the Madison Heights house was Carolyn's full-time home. We continued dating steady but we did not live together for what would be quite a few years. Over the next few years Carolyn and I shared many experiences that we had in common. A few more memorable events included skiing trips to Colorado, Tahoe and Vermont, boating on Lake St. Clair and trips to Las Vegas. One of the trips to Vegas resulted in buying a time-share at the Flamingo Hilton, which we used twice a year and also for TEAM customer entertaining.

Once TEAM Resources was established and successful, I suggested that Carolyn quit her job at Modern Engineering and join TEAM as our personnel manager. This would be an increase in salary and career advancement for her. She would be in charge of employee benefit plans, visa documentation and managing our office. She would also be a big help in organizing our annual picnic and the holiday entertainment at the DAC and also at the Skyline Club in Southfield. As part of TEAM Carolyn was indispensable.

The Conrad's Move to Fairfield Glade, Tennessee

Elmer and Geraldine, Carolyn's Mom and Dad decide to move from Walled Lake, MI to Fairfield Glade, TN. Elmer liked to travel and often he took car trips to places of interest. Geraldine's close-cousin Meredith & Dan had recently bought a new house in Fairfield Glade, Tennessee. Dan was an avid golfer and Fairfield has 5 championship courses. Elmer planned a trip to visit them and see the new house. Geraldine and Elmer were very impressed with this resort community. Fairfield Glade, known for its outstanding golf courses and temperate climate is in the foothills of the Smokey Mountains.

After spending their entire life in the Walled Lake area; it was time to consider retirement. Fairfield Glade appeared to be a wise choice. They bought a new model home located on the fairway of the Druid Hills golf course. This wooded location offered a panoramic view that was maintained by the resort.

Fairfield Glade was an attraction for vacationers and an offered condominium unit time-shares as well as new housing development. They had a clubhouse, pool, tennis courts and a first-class restaurant. Horseback riding was also a popular activity. The Glade is relatively close to the town of Crossville, for shopping and restaurants. Knoxville is the largest nearby city and it is only 75 miles from Fairfield Glade.

Their retirement decision turned out to be a welcome asset for the entire Conrad family. Carolyn and I visited them on a number of occasions, especially holiday weekends. These were like mini-vacations and included the car-ride thru the various states coming and going.

Most of these visits included Carolyn's brothers and families. We had many memorable experiences. I especially remember the dinners at the clubhouse and the entertainment. For example the band would play "Rocky-top Tennessee" and the waitresses would join in the dancing. Another memory was the stage-shows at the Cumberland Playhouse with her family. We also took trips to Gatlinburg, Pigeon Forge and the Smokey Mountain village of Rugby to explore the craft-shows; where I bought a few hand- sewn teddy bears. Elmer and Geraldine spent the next 10 years in retirement at their home in Fairfield Glade.

Carolyn and the Bearded Collies

Ever since I met Carolyn my life was shared with her shaggy-dogs. Dog showing and breeding is Carolyn's passion. When we first met Carolyn had 2-dogs, Marnie & Shan plus a white kitten. Over the years our lifestyle was dedicated to the dogs! My first experience was when Carolyn bred a litter of Beardie puppies. This litter included 4 puppies, male/female mix. She sold 2 and kept 2 for herself. We were still dating and I wanted to keep a special puppy for myself. We had named this unusual puppy "Teddy Blue Bear", because his coat and eyes were blue, which is relatively rare for this breed. She said I could keep a puppy but I wanted to pay the full asking price of $500.00 to help her pay bills. So I bought my Teddy Bear. He would live with me in the condo-on-Lake St. Clair. This puppy was like a magnet for meeting people, mostly girls.

I would bathe-him on a Saturday and/or Sunday morning and walk him on a leash to the park on the pathway to the rest-area to brush-him-out. I was inundated by single-lady joggers, wanting to pet Teddy and ask questions about Teddy and his daddy; like where does Teddy live and where is his mommy. I had to respond that we were both single. Teddybear was certainly worth what I paid for him!

In following years I would join Carolyn at many dog-shows around the country. Actually, our "honeymoon" was in Sonoma, California where the National Bearded Collie Specialty was being held. I recall that we attended major dog shows in Atlanta, Orlando, Baltimore, and Omaha, Kennebunkport and Stratford, Ontario as well as numerous local shows.

Carolyn does both the training and the showing of her dogs. She has won many major trophies, awards and ribbons. Recently Shawnee won "Best Veteran" dog at the Canadian Bearded Collie National 2-years in a row.

Her most famous Beardie is Delilah who won "Best of Winners" in the National show at Fort Collins, Colorado. Very sadly, as I was writing this book our Delilah passed on to the "Rainbow Bridge", just days before her 15th birthday. She will always be remembered. Delilah was very special in many ways. Her accomplishments at Bearded Collie dog shows were recognized by the 'Beardie-world of breeders, trainers and competitor owners. Carolyn was responsible for Delilah's training and handling. Claudia McNulty, a premier breeder said "Delilah gave us the ride of a lifetime". She finished with terrific wins, including the WB & Bow at the 2004 BCCA National Specialty and WB BOW & BOS at the National Capital Specialty. This beautiful Beardie was also a multiple group winner as well as gaining Obedience and Agility titles. Currently we have 3-Beardies, Shawnee, Petunia and Fudge.

Carolyn's latest litter had two special puppies. Fudge's coat is dark-brown and his brother Mackinaw is black-with white features, therefore the pair were named after Mackinaw Fudge. These two puppies were spectacular hits at public craft-shows and in downtown walks. Mackinaw now lives in New York near West Point with a special person. Carolyn is training Fudge in agility (running, jumping hurdles, weaving poles and tunnels, etc.). He lives with the other 2 girls.

A Surprise Phone Call in Spring 1991

On a Sunday afternoon Carolyn and I were relaxing at my condo on Lake St. Clair when the phone rang. I answered it and a female voice asked if I was Arthur Hoffmann. I said yes I am. She said, "Something like do you know a woman named Celine"? "Yes", I replied. She said, "I'm Elaine and I'm married to your son Art". I was dumbfounded! It was like a miracle. My prayers were answered!

When I last saw baby Arthur he was 13 months-old and barely walking. At the time I was visiting him at Celine's house in Westland, MI and had brought him a few toys to play with. I still remember him being very playful and happy. I did not know then, that I may never see or hear about baby Arthur again! He would disappear out of my life; until now! Elaine's phone call was a Godsend.

Art Jr. was now 35 years old and we would now be forever reunited. Over the years I worried and prayed that Art Jr. was well and hopefully happy. My Mom and Dad would often ask if I heard anything. He was their first grandson and mom had cared for him as a baby and became attached and concerned about his health and safety.

The phone call lasted for what seemed like an eternity. We talked for a long while and I found out that they lived in California near Disneyland. Art & Elaine had been married for quite a while and had two-little-boys, Joel and Alan. Arthur was employed as a technical writer, (must run in the family). Elaine was a teacher. I also have to thank Elaine's mother, Mariam because she was the person that instigated the search for Arthur's father. The only fortunate part of this story is that Celine kept the Hoffmann surname for Art, even though Celine would remarry again in the future.

I was anxious to see my new family. Carolyn was familiar with my past and she also was excited to share in this great news. Art Jr and Elaine and family made plans to visit Carolyn and me during the coming "Fourth-of-July" holiday. In the mean time we would exchange letters and photos.

I immediately contacted my family and relayed the news. They also were very interested because this news completed a long-missing chapter in our family's history.

When the "Fourth-of July" reunion event arrived all of our family members were included for the festive occasion. The get-together included Steve & Kim, Brother George, Chuck & Mary Bonten family, Liz & Lowell Wolfe, Richard & Meg Hoffmann (Florida), Rick & Billy Hoffmann. It was a dream come-true and a real God-send because July 4th was also my mother's birthday!

I only wish Mom & Dad were there. They would have been so proud and happy. We were joining our separate Hoffmann families together in way that would become inseparable in the future. We would all visit, communicate and celebrate life events with one another in coming years. I am very thankful for this fortunate outcome. As this storytelling continues there will be other revelations.

New House at 34045 Jefferson Avenue, St. Clair Shores, Michigan

While I continued living at the high-rise condominium I was constantly looking for a nice parcel of property on Lake St. Clair with the intention of building a new house. The idea was that a nice house on the lake would improve my lifestyle as a homeowner and be a good investment for the future. One day it came to pass. Driving down Jefferson Avenue in St. Clair Shores a "house for sale" sign was just posted. This house was previously sold, but the sale fell-thru. The listing realtor lived across the street, so I stopped-in to see the vacant house and property. She showed me around and explained the previous sale and the current asking price.

The house was considered a tear-down due to its age, condition and multi-level layout and homeowner add-ons. The current owner had moved to Florida and she was anxious sell. The property was very nice with 90 feet of Lake Frontage, a steel sea-wall and boat hoist. I had been watching for an opportunity and lakefront sales were relatively rare, especially for a nice property. I told the realtor that it was definitely a tear-down for me and there would be extra expenses involved. However I did like the property. I made an offer at $10,000 below the current listing, but it was contingent on a quick no-hassle firm sale. The realtor called the owner with the information and my offer was accepted. I made a large deposit and assumed a 1-year land contract for the remainder. This was not a pre-planned event so now I had to get a new house plan and find a builder.

I had not discussed this new house and property idea with anyone so it was a big surprise to Kim, who was living with me and to Carolyn also. This project would consume me for the next year.

I did find a good private builder that was very helpful. Keith Camps reviewed the property and old house for the tear down issues, gave me a fair estimate with change contingencies and a lot of valuable advice. He recommended Dale Studnicka, a young architect that was familiar with the latest building and materials technology. We discussed various type- of-house plans and decided on a modified story-and-half that would reflect a French Manor theme. The exterior of the house was a premium white split-rock brick with "drivet" architectural features. This home would have a full-extra-deep basement with a walk-out access feature. The main floor was designed with spacious rooms and built for entertaining. It turned out to be a very attractive house and the hope was that it would increase in value, especially since it was right on Lake St. Clair. I had bought this property as-is in July 1995 and by August 1996 the new house was completed and ready for occupancy. This beautiful home did appreciate and after 10 years it was appraised for about $1.1 million.

However, when it finally sold in 2008 the economy and housing market was in deep recession. At that point I had lost virtually all of my gain in equity. As it turned out we lived in this house for 10 years and I did recover our initial investment.

While I was in the process of planning the new house and before the demolition of the old house, Kim was using the existing house as a party-house. Every weekend Kim and her friends would entertain and use this house as a private resort on the lake. Finally, the old house was demolished in one-day and all the debris removed prior to the new construction.

Once the construction started I would follow the progress almost daily. Kim and I lived in the condo and Carolyn continued to live in the Madison Heights house. Once the new house was completely rough-in with all of the rooms identified I decided to do something special.

I set-up a folding-table in the dining area, that had a panoramic view-of-Lake Saint Clair. I decorated the table with a tablecloth, candle and a bottle of champagne. I then picked-up Carolyn for our Saturday night date. I did not tell her what was planned for this evening, so it would be a surprise. I had ordered a pizza and we had a romantic dinner as the Sun was setting over the lake. I told her that when we move-in together we could plan our wedding and reception at the sea-wall on the lake.

The Wedding of Art & Carolyn – September 13, 1997

Carolyn and her friends had been planning the wedding and reception for quite a while and it was an elaborate affair. We had about 110 guests and all of the activities, planned and catered by exclusive vendors. Rev. David Huseltine, Carolyn's pastor at St. Johns' Methodist Church in Royal Oak presided the marriage vows. Marilyn was "maid-of-honor", George was "best man" and Cally, Carolyn's Bearded-Collie dog, was the "flower girl". The ceremony was outside at the seawall-on-the-lake during a beautiful sunny afternoon.

The entertainment included Rennie Kaufmann on the 'keyboard" and a rendition of romantic songs by Alison Peck, an accomplished soloist. The food was provided by the "Canape Cart", chef-cuisine. It was a very memorable event.

Living on Lake St. Clair

Carolyn and I would live in this house-on-the-lake for the next 10 years while we both worked at the TEAM Resources office in Auburn Hills. The Jefferson house was ideal for entertaining customers and personal friends. TEAM sponsored annual picnics and special events, such as the Fourth of July, fire-works party for both family and employees. The fireworks barge was docked in front of the St. Clair Shores park just down-the-street from us. We had a "birds-eye-view" for seeing and listening. This event was very popular with hundreds of boats anchored just out front of our house. Living on the lake allowed for many unique experiences, including boating to restaurants, sunsets, swimming and rough weather action.

The Wedding of Kimberly & Robert Bloink --July 29, 2000

July 29, 2000 was a perfect summer day for this happy occasion. The wedding took place at "Christ the King Lutheran Church in Grosse Pointe Woods, Michigan. The reception was at the Grosse Pointe War Memorial on Lake St. Clair. The wedding ceremony was beautiful and serene inside this traditional church setting. The reception was held outside on the colorful landscaped gardens and sculptured surroundings of the War Memorial grounds. The entire Hoffmann / Bloink clan were in attendance. Everyone dressed in their finest attire. Art and Elaine from California, Marilyn and Louis from Phoenix, Rich and Meg from Florida and Wally from Houston, Texas were all in attendance.

There was dinner and dancing inside the splendid hall. The tables were immaculately decorated and the four-tiered wedding cake was elaborate and delicious. I know all this because I paid for much of it.

The David & Clarke Bonten Wedding

Another memorable event occurred just one year following Kim and Robert Bloink's nuptials. Dave and Clarke tied the knot in Lexington, Kentucky on July 21, 2001and the entire extended family was invited. For us it was like a mini-vacation to travel down to Kentucky for the 2-day wedding and reception. We stayed overnight at the Shaker Village at Pleasant Hill and enjoyed the experience.

The wedding and reception was at the Bodley-Billoc House that had a unique setting. The actual ceremony was in a private outside patio that was secluded and personal. I remember that it was a very hot sunny summer day and I forgot to wear a hat and sun-glasses.

Clarke also has an interesting story to tell. She is the great granddaughter of Eddie Rickenbacker; the

World War I flying ace and Medal-of-Honor recipient. Essentially he was the "Red Baron" of the U.S. I'm sure "Snoppy" would remember him, but Eddie & the "Red Baron" never met on the battlefield. Her father, Brian, is the executive-director of the famous Overbrook Farms in Lexington, Kentucky and he organized the wedding agenda.

While it was a very nice wedding and ceremony, the most interesting event was a bus-guided-tour of the Overbrook horse farm. We were allowed to view the entire grounds, starting at the actual breeding barn, horse stables, track-workout and the very secure fenced-in area where the stud breed baby-horses (foals) are corralled. Each foal had an ear-tag that identified the owner and other information. At that time, Overbrook Farms owned "Storm Cat", the most famous stud stallion in America. The typical stud fee for his services started at $500,000 per job. In the future, whenever George and I went to the "races" we always bet on every horse that had Storm Cat breeding or the term "Cat" in their name.

The Blue King – Children's Christmas Adventure Story Book Background

When the soccer leagues were first organized in Rochester, Michigan, the little boys and girls were placed on the same team. This appeared to be a big advantage for the boys.

Kimberly came home one afternoon after playing soccer. She was very upset and disappointed with her soccer team. Whenever Kim got a chance to score, the goalie would just grab the slow-moving ball and throw it back. She was a good athlete and a fast runner and this was very discouraging for her

Well, to console her we made-up a bedtime story about *a little girl, who became the best soccer player on an all-boys team.* This was a night-to-night continuing chapter-to-chapter story. I would make-up this tale as we lay on her canopy-bed until she fell-asleep.

The story would continue the next evening when I resumed the tale. This night time story was entitled "The Blue King". In later years (2003) I embellished and completed this fanciful tale as a published children's storybook. This accomplishment became an obsession and legacy for me.

The "Blue King" storybook took on a life of its own. After writing the story I wanted to have it published as an illustrated children's book. I felt that the story carried a good message that could inspire young children to practice friendship, understanding and niceness (FUN); using the Santa Claus mythology to reflect "giving", and not receiving.

My first challenge was to find an illustrator-artist to convey the story in a manner that would attract children and provide excitement and curiosity to the climax. I attended a nearby art-fair in Grosse Pointe looking for a potential artist. Several artists recommended Lynn Morgan, a gifted artist and musician. I approached him and his wife Linda with my book proposal and they expressed interest. The art-show was just closing and I invited him to my home to discuss my project. I gave Lynn a copy of my manuscript with some very crude sketches I had made and he agreed to read it and respond. Within 2 weeks I received a package in the mail containing a full-color illustration of a key-image for the book. I was flabbergasted with his work. I immediately called him and said I wanted him to do the entire book in whatever fashion he felt necessary to convey the story... I asked him for a quote and I accepted it right away.

Lynn Morgan is a very special person. He is both an artist and a musician who creates his art images and his musical compositions with great enthusiasm. Realizing at a young age that God had given him creative gifts Lynn began to develop these abilities through years of study and practice. His award winning art images have been enjoyed by collectors around the world and his songs have touched the hearts of thousands of listening fans. Lynn Morgan has been inducted into the Michigan Hall of Fame, due to his "country-music" awards and accomplishments.

Lynn took a break from his realistic approached to painting to do the whimsical illustrations in "The Blue King" that are an example of his versatility. Lynn Morgan feels it was fun to bring the tale of The Blue King, to life through his illustrations. He hopes everyone will enjoy the adventure as you and your child become whisked away to the "Blue Kingdom".

During the publishing phase of "The Blue King" storybook, Lynn Morgan suggested that he would like to compose an original song to sing the praises of this unique children's story. I agreed and this is became a very special enhancement of the storybook. Lynn is an accomplished vocalist, with an amazing voice and the gift of whistling. He sang and whistled the lyrics of this wonderful children's song.

The book was published by the "Millbrook Printing Company", Grand Ledge, Michigan, a premier color production firm. The published book included the imbedded song and the narrated story on a CD. The song and music were recorded at "Big Bear Productions", Midland Michigan. The entire "Blue King" project was "pure Michigan". All participants, including the author, artist, composer, printer, music production, children's choir, CD and narration were based in Michigan. The initial production was 7,500 copies in 2003. The ISBN # 0-9742967-0-8 and copies of the original publication may still be available on Amazon.

Over the years I entered and sold the book at book-fairs around the country. I visited many schools and created a power-point presentation. I also donated large numbers of books to various charities, including the Katrina storm victims, Kiwanis Clubs, Toys-for-Tots and the Rotary. Actually I donated the remainder of my inventory, 4,000 books to the Traverse City Rotary Club for Christmas distribution in 2015. The result of this donation was an invitation to join this very special Rotary Group. I have been an active member ever since.

Recently I have pursued the idea of finding a movie-maker to consider production of a "Blue King" children's film. I envision the potential film to resemble the "Polar Express" movie that has become a traditional Holiday showing. The Polar Express production is a life-like animation with Tom Hanks adding the narration.

Children's movies are a huge box-office draw; especially at Christmas time. A "Blue King" film would reflect a "North to South Pole" children's adventure story, while creating several unique new characters that would become an annual Holiday event. The "Blue King / Santa Claus", relationship is intended to inspire children/ (adults) to pursue universal, friendship, understanding and niceness (FUN) in our troubled world.

A review of recent children's movies indicate, potential total monetary revenues, including box-office & merchandizing, of over $1 billion dollars!

Recently I have created several social-media sites to expose and market "The Blue King" storybook that I believe has movie production potential. Interested parties are invited to visit the Internet and social-media for information using key-words: The Blue King, blue king, blue king story, blue king home, etc. on Facebook, Instagram, you tube, twitter, and google+. You can also access **www.blueking.net** and view the DVD Song & Story and also print out the complete "The Blue King" storybook as an E-book for FREE in full-color.

I have also committed a portion of any Blue King movie royalties to Traverse City Rotary Charities or other "good works" charity organizations.

Family Relationships and Activities

Growing up in the Hoffmann family was a very fortunate experience for all of us. Mom and Dad were a great example of proper parenting for us to follow. As children, we all lived happily together, without any jealousy or animosity toward one-another. In fact we played and enjoyed being together. As our family grew-up into adulthood, we all pursued individual lifestyles and continued to share our experiences at family get-togethers. We have numerous memories of these occasions. Our now separate families have shared in holding these special birthday, holiday, parties at the various homes. I remember Mom and Dad being present at all of these events over many years. These memories included visits to the homes of: Mary & Chuck Bonten, Liz & Lowell Wolfe, Kim & Robert Bloink, Art & Carolyn Hoffmann, Clarke & David at their Rochester home, and most recently Bill Hoffmann for Thomas's 1st birthday party.

An especially memorable Christmas get-together was at Liz and Lowell's house when Carolyn was surprised to receive a brand new trail bike as a Christmas gift. Chuck Bonten still owned the Village Cyclery and Carolyn was relatively new to our family. This gift was a welcome to our family gesture.

My Eightieth Birthday Celebration

August 3, 2016 was my 80th birthday event at George's condo community hall. For me it was a very special occasion. Kim made all of the arrangements and Carolyn and I drove down from Traverse City. All of the local family members attended. Art & Elaine from California and Marilyn & Lewis Astroth, from Phoenix also came. Albert & Pat Flamme also attended. Albert was my childhood friend from the old Detroit neighborhood. It was a great opportunity for everyone to get further acquainted.

Of special interest was the entertainment. We were honored to experience Clarke's violin concertino of her very talented children. The four-member violinists' group are little Alice, Isabelle, Charles and Clarke. They played several arrangements of pleasing harmonic melodies as a group and also several solos by each of them. The audience was mesmerized by these young musicians; each of them had their own violin to fit their age.

What is very interesting is that Clarke is a music teacher that utilizes the "Suzuai" method of teaching violin for children. She has used this method to instruct her children to play and read music. All three children are members of the Oakland Youth Orchestra (OYO) and each one of them specializes in the various strings, philharmonic or symphony music.

Our family members often do things together and plan events. We always attend the children's activities, picnics and recently we went to a Detroit Tiger evening game and dinner in the Detroit's farmers' market-place.

Individual Personal Achievements

Another interesting aspect of our family members is the individual achievements of members of the Hoffmann extended family.

- <u>Richard (Rich) P. Hoffmann, BS (Pharmacy), PharmD.</u> Is the youngest member of the Hoffmann Family. He graduated from Wayne State University with a Bachelor's Degree and Doctorate in Pharmacy. During his pharmacy career he was Director of Pharmacy at the notable St. Joseph Mercy Hospital in Pontiac, MI. for 13 years. Rich was also on the Adjunct Faculty of Wayne State University and Ferris State College for many years. In addition, he has authored over 2,500 pharmacy-related publications including 10 books and a weekly "Ask the Pharmacist" newspaper column which he has continued for many years. Currently, he serves as a Consumer and Patient Representative for various Food & Drug Administration (FDA) Advisory Committees. My Brother Richard is also a Research Advocate for the Parkinson's Foundation, along with his wife Margaret (Meg).

- <u>Kimberly & Robert Bloink, are both Attorney's</u> and practice Civil & Contract Law as well as Tax and Investment Consulting. Their daughter (my granddaughter) Abigail Faye attends the Cranbrook Schools, in Birmingham, MI. She is an outstanding student with a bright future ahead.

- <u>Charles (Chuck) Bonten,</u> is a Michigan State University graduate with a BA-Accounting. He started his career working in the bicycle sales and service industry and owned the Village Cyclery in Grosse Pointe, MI. When skateboards became popular, Chuck established a new business, marketing and assembling skateboards to special order. Owning his own outlet, and with the Internet connection his business increased greatly. TGM Skateboards is now the largest skateboard dealer on both eBay and also Amazon.

- <u>David & Clarke Bonten,</u> David is an MSU graduate with a BA-Accounting, but he earned his MBA at the University of Michigan. He is also a Certified Public Accountant (CPA). David is now the President & CFO of TGM Skateboards. Clarke (Rickenbacker) Bonten is an accomplished violinist and outstanding music teacher.

- <u>Eric Bonten</u>, also is a MSU graduate with Bachelor Degrees in Finance, History and Philosophy- with Ancient Greek & Latin majors. Eric also speaks German, French, Spanish and Italian. He has lived in Berlin, Germany for many years and owns his own European skateboard company similar to his dad Chuck.

What is of particular interest is that recently Eric obtained his German Citizenship status and passport. This qualifies him for dual-U.S. & German citizen rights and privileges. Since Germany is part of the European Union, the citizen's privileges are expanded to all of the European Union countries.

The reason Eric was qualified to accomplish this dual-citizenship is due to our Mom & Dad's relationship. At the time of marriage, (June 9, 1932), Dad was a German citizen and Mom was a Polish citizen. Therefore, all of the children born in the U.S. prior to 1947 were American citizens, but they were eligible for German citizenship as well. This was based on German law and Dad's citizenship. Currently all of the Hoffmann children (George, Arthur Mary, Elizabeth and Walter) qualify (Richard was born in 1948 and is exempted). Of course this qualification is based on an extensive application, similar to Eric's pursuit. The advantage of having the dual German citizen status also allows the children of the recipient to also qualify. This would qualify for passport travel and educational benefits within Germany and the European Union. Kimberly Bloink is currently pursuing applications for herself, Abigail and me.

- <u>William (Bill) Hoffmann</u>, Bill (Brother Richard's 2nd son) followed a career in law enforcement. He is now a senior Police Officer in the Holly, Michigan police department. Officer Hoffmann received a special award in 2008 for bravery. While on patrol he witnessed a vehicle that had lost control and was submerged in a local lake. He then attempted to rescue the driver, but to no avail. Bill and Ruschell have a son, Thomas Hoffmann, born March 16, 2017.

- <u>Arthur W. Hoffmann, Ed.D., P.E.</u> – The author's background is in mechanical engineering. He graduated from Wayne State University with a BSME In 1970. In 1970 Art received his certification as a Professional Engineer for the State of Michigan # 18418. In pursuing years he graduated from Central Michigan University with a MA Degree in Supervision & Management. Following the MA, he attended Western Michigan University and earned a Doctorate Degree in Educational Leadership (Ed.D.). Arthur's accomplishments includes:

  a. Development of the 1ˢᵗ dynamically-tested child safety seat. This CRS was marketed as the GM Love Seat in 1967;
  b. Developed the anti-submarine seat-cushion ramp – 1ˢᵗ Booster Seat;
  c. Collapsible Energy-Absorbing (E/A) automotive interior structure;
  d. Author of "The Blue King", children's' Christmas storybook;
  e. The "Don't be a Dummy" and "Precious Cargo" safety-primer books;
  f. Several patents related to automotive mechanical components.

Moving to Traverse City, Michigan

Over the years, Carolyn and I had spent time visiting the Grand Traverse area where Carolyn competed in the annual dog-shows in Traverse City. We also visited Louis & Marilyn in their condo at the Homestead Resort on Lake Michigan. We thought Traverse City and Northern Michigan would be an ideal area we should consider for future retirement. It offered a lifestyle that fit our interests in summer and winter activities and had all of the amenities for entertainment, recreation, shopping, and of course health care facilities.

While Carolyn was dog-showing, I spent time looking at the real-estate and housing market. In particular I liked visiting the annual "parade-of-homes" open houses.

On one of these visits I discovered, what I believed was a house-model and location that fit our needs and future lifestyle. The Incochee Woods development is located on Wayne Hill, offering direct views of the West Bay of Lake Michigan, adjacent to downtown Traverse City. Our property is at the top-of-the-Incochee parcel and borders Hickory Meadows and the Leelanau County line.

Our parcel contains about 1-1/2 acres, which includes a large, fenced-in, front-yard for the dogs, a hill-side vineyard, a rear-walk-out patio & yard, with a flowing water-scape. The house is a 3,000 sq.ft., craftsman-style ranch, with a full-basement and 2-attached-garages with total-space to accommodate 3-vehicles. Our property is completely wooded on-all- sides and we have foot-trails into the woods that the deer also access.

Carolyn has established protected areas where she has planted and cultivated local and Northwest Michigan wild flowers. These include "Lady-Slippers", Jack-in-the-Pulpit, Trillium, Redbud and Michigan Holly that are identified and screened-in for protection against deer trampling or feeding.

One of my hobbies is to feed the wildlife in my backyard. I have built and erected several feeding platforms for the deer, rabbits, squirrels, possum, fox, raccoons, etc. I have several types of bird houses and feeders for a wide variety of feathered friends.

Traverse City and this Northern Michigan area offer a variety of unique sport and fun activities. Residents and guests can enjoy natural wonders such as the National Park Sand Dunes for hiking, climbing and self-guided scenic car tours and concerts on the sandy-hills.

Another popular activity is tubing on the Platte River in rafts, canoes or floats. The continuous-current carries you downward in the shallow river from Platte Lake in the warm-summer-water for a nice-long trip that merges directly into chilly Lake Michigan that takes your breath-away. Following the water-ride you can picnic on the grass or sand and also hunt for unique Petoskey stones.

The West and East Bays of Lake Michigan border downtown Traverse City with the long-narrow Mission Peninsula being the natural dividing-line between the East-West Bays. Mission Peninsula is a haven for vineyards and wineries that blanket the property on both sides. The Peninsula drive route is considered one of the top ten scenic drives in the U.S.

Northern Michigan is also a winter wonderland featuring skiing, snow-boarding, connecting snow-mobile routes and facilities thru-out the entire area. Top skiing resorts dot the area; such as Boyne Mountain and Highlands, Nobs-Nob, Schuss Mountain, Shanty-Creek, Crystal Mountain, and others that are local and within an hours-drive.

When I think of skiing, I had an interesting experience recently. I received a phone call from a childhood playmate that I hadn't heard from in 50 years. Albert Flamme and I grew-up in the old Detroit neighborhood as children. We went to school together, and we are both engineers. However, we lost contact in later years. Al turned out to also be a ski instructor and a member of the local ski-patrol. He had called me out-of-the-blue, and asked if I still ski. I said yes, and I also now live in Traverse City close to several ski-resorts. We made plans to ski together in the coming week. He drove-up for the weekend, and we skied 3 days at "Schuss Mountain" and spent our spare-time doing wine-tasting at the many wineries. We now plan to ski regularly. Al's wife Pat & Carolyn got acquainted and we all plan to visit each other as often as possible.

Traverse City is also the home for several "Tall-Ships" at the "Discovery Pier" harbor. These sailing ships offer day and twilight tours around the bay. The "Manitou" also schedules over-night cruises that include sleeping-quarters and breakfast cooked on-board.

These are some of the life-style attractions that influenced our move to Northern Michigan. Since we moved here in 2008, the Grand Traverse region has continued its fast-growth. The Munson Medical Center has expanded immensely. Cherry Capitol Airport has also expanded; adding direct flights to major hubs. The airport is very convenient to access, since it is only about 3 miles from our house and the downtown area. Traverse City is also the home of the U.S. Coast Guard. In the summer season the greater Traverse Bay area is a vacation destination becoming Michigan's second largest city in the summer and known as a "foodie town".

The Traverse City Rotary Club

In 2015 I donated my remaining inventory of 4,000 copies of the "The Blue King" storybook to the Traverse City Rotary Club. These books were distributed to the various Rotary clubs and children's charities throughout Michigan and the Midwest. The book was published in 2003 and I was not interested in selling the remaining books but I wanted to promote the storyline because of its meaningful message of Friendship, Understanding and Niceness (FUN); that I believed would be inspirational for young children. This make-believe tale emulates the Santa Claus / Christmas theme coupled with an interesting adventurous twist that would appeal to young children the world-over.

Currently I am promoting this children's storybook on social media to expose the storyline that I believe has the potential for becoming a movie that could be a children's Holiday feature.

The TC Rotary Club has the recognition of being the world's wealthiest Rotary club due to the foresight of purchasing both the Boy Scout and Girl Scout campsites back in the early 1920's. In the 1970's oil was discovered on the Boy Scout property and the monetary revenues have funded the TC Rotary "good works" foundation ever since.

Traverse City is the home of 3 Rotary clubs; Sunrise, Noon and Twilight organizations. The Noon club has about 250 members and meets every Tuesday's at 12:00 pm.

1. Since I joined the Traverse City Rotary Club in 2015 I have been involved in some interesting activities. I was first involved in the 2015 Rotary Show as a "flasher" (trench-coat & all), complementing the Grand Traverse area "Public Art Appreciation" contributions. Other activities included several events in which I participated;

2. I also am a member of the "Precision (folding-lawn chair) Drill-Team" for the annual Cherry-Festival parade. (similar to brief-case event in other parades);

3. Served as a member of Rotary Grant committees for local charities;

4. I was the "catcher w/jock-strap" for the "Flying Walnettos" Rotary Show circus act. I also built the teeter-totter equipment;

5. I dressed as coalminer to celebrate the Rotary purchase of the "Discovery Pier". This area was the location of the former Marathon Oil Company coal docks and storage. The property parcel includes the deepest harbor on this side of Lake Michigan. This pier is now the home port for several "tall-sailing ships".

   I dug-up buried coal on the property and packaged "Embryonic Diamond" souvenirs as a fund-raiser for local charities' 'Good Works'.

6. I am also involved as an advisor for high-school career counseling.

In 2003 I published a book entitled "Jobs-Apprentice 101-An American Solution, creating jobs, entrepreneurs & reducing poverty". (ISBN 978-1-4759-3132-7, pub., I Universe, 2003).

This book was based on my experience with TEAM Resources, Inc. and lessons learned through job opportunities, training, and a concern to improve employment opportunity for inner-city and rural-area youths. I have donated copies to high schools, libraries and teachers for reference. I also assist in career-day activities at local schools. Recently, I was approved, and have a teaching certificate in Michigan as a substitute as needed.

The California Hoffmann Family

Over the years, after I found out that I had a surprise family living in California, we would have many get-togethers. Not only would Carolyn & I visit and communicate with Art Jr. & Elaine but all of our family members would as well. Chuck & Mary Bonten would visit them whenever they were in LA. Kim & Robert Bloink would do likewise. As for me I am so pleased and proud of all of our family members, on both sides that have accepted this re-union of Art Jr. and me. We have enjoyed each other's company and I have nice memories.

Watching the two-little boys, Joel and Alan grow-up has been an especially rewarding experience. I can remember the boys in their band outfits and their instruments as they made their way through the school years. I wish to thank Elaine & Art for their upbringing, education and the bright future they have ahead of them. Mariam & Charles Arnold Post, Elaine's mom & dad, also played a big part in Joel & Alan's growing-up.

Joel & Jacquie Hoffmann Wedding: October 9, 2009

Attending Joel and Jacquie's wedding was a milestone for me because it would engender the next generation. I could become a great-grandfather? Jackie planned the entire wedding including all of the table decorations and souvenirs. The wedding and reception was held at "The Turnip Rose" assembly hall in Newport Beach, CA. I was a wonderful affair and we considered it a mini-vacation as we spent additional time traveling in California.

Carolyn & I and Kim, Robert and baby Abigail Bloink attended the wedding ceremony and the following reception. This wedding would have a profound effect on me as the years went on. Joel and Jacquie Hoffmann make a great couple. They both are very talented in what they do. Joel has been working and learning the movie/film business and making video-trailer productions. I believe his experience at 'Disney Land' had a lot to prepare him for the entertainment industry. Jacquie is especially talented in the visual arts, painting and decorating. She is also an "event- planner" as a business pursuit.

Since their wedding in 2009, the Joel & Jacquie Hoffmann family has grown to five members. Nathaniel born January 22, 2013 was my first Great-Grand Child. He recently celebrated his 5th birthday. His party was a "Star Wars" extravaganza, with the entire house and outside yard covered with Star Wars displays, models, video and a live fencing-demonstration.

Mikey born on September 5, 2014 reminds me of my family. My brother George was 2-years older than me. Similar to Nathan & Mikey; George & I were always doing things together and inseparable.

As I'm writing this memoir we received a big surprise with little Evangeline Rose, born on March 7, 2018. Little Eva Rose is the joy of all of the Hoffmann affiliated families. The boys are O.K., but girls are special! She is a beautiful baby; and my first great-granddaughter.

Side note: The Joel-Jacquie wedding reception was also important for me personally, since it would be an opportunity for me to once again see Celine.

Art Jr.'s mom, Celine was present at the front of the reception line. I had not seen or heard from her in over fifty-years. She hardly noticed me, but she did briefly shake-my-hand. During the reception neither she nor I made any effort to communicate. Our table was located at the opposite side of the room from her and her relatives. I regret that we did not talk but it was an awkward situation. However another opportunity to communicate would present itself in the future.

In 2016 I received a note in the mail from Celine. Her note said she was sorry and wanted to apologize for her action and the hurt she inflicted. I replied to her short note and I accepted her apology. I don't harbor any animosity toward her but I was not the only person that was affected.

Over the years I had constantly hoped and prayed that little Arthur was safe and alright. My mom and dad often asked if I've heard anything of Arthur. They had become attached to the baby because they watched over him at our house while Celine went back to work after our separation. I only wish that Elaine and her mom could have found me sooner. The surprise call from Elaine was in the spring of 1990. My mom passed away October 17, 1985 of a drug-overdose in the hospital. My dad died one-year later.

Lifestyle Memories and Events

Over the years Carolyn and I enjoyed a personal lifestyle that was not related to our work or other commitments. As a couple we had a lot in common with Louis and Marilyn and planned trips and vacation time together.

Louis and Marilyn had moved to Phoenix, Arizona where Louis was offered a job opportunity. This arrangement resulted in long-distance travel between Michigan and Arizona. The Astroth's also owned a condo on Lake Michigan at the Homestead Resort where they spent their summers.

Carolyn and I also moved from St. Clair Shores to Traverse City. This move created a separation from friends and family so we had to travel back & forth for special holidays or family events.

All of us enjoyed skiing and we made several trips to Colorado, Tahoe and Whistler, Ontario. We also took several cruise ship vacations to the Caribbean and Alaska. During the summers we did a lot of things together.

Louis & Marilyn's son Kurt went to college at Arizona State in Tucson. He had joined the ROTC and upon graduation he enlisted in the U.S. Navy. Kurt was often stationed in San Diego.

On one of our trips to Phoenix, we all drove down to San Diego to see Kurt and his friend Jen. For us it was a sight-seeing trip and a mini-vacation. We were able to see the naval-base and some of the other attractions. Not too soon afterwards we would go to San Diego again.

Kurt & Jen Astroth Wedding – San Diego – February 18, 2017

When Carolyn & I received the invitation for the coming wedding we made plans for the entire week of events. Marilyn had made a reservation for a large rental property that would accommodate the whole wedding party. Carolyn & I, Louis & Marilyn, Dave & Betty Conrad and Jennifer's Mom occupied this house. Dan & Connie Conrad chose to stay at a hotel, but would join us at the rental during the day. It was a Conrad family gathering and we all got to know each other better and we helped organize the pre-wedding party at Kurt & Jen's house. Louis's daughters and families also attended the wedding ceremony and reception.

Son Art & Joel, with his little boys, Nathan & Mikey, along with, Alan & friend Annie, drove-down from LA to visit us. We did some sight-seeing and toured the aircraft carrier "Midway" and a WWII submarine. They did not attend the wedding but we were able spend time together. They all came to the rental house for a long visit before they had to return to LA.

On the Friday before the wedding we attended the rehearsal dinner at "Tom Ham's Lighthouse" on Harbor Island which is a popular destination for naval station personnel.

The wedding was a military-style affair with the groom and his entourage dressed in formal U.S. Navy Officer uniform dress. The wedding ceremony was at "First United Methodist Church in San Diego, CA. Following the ceremony the new Bride & Groom were acknowledged as they, passed-thru the tunnel-of-crossed-swords, presented by the Navy Honor Guard.

The wedding reception was held at the "World Famous I-Bar" on the Naval Air Station on North Island, Coronado. The entire wedding party attended as well as well as Kurt's many friends and fellow officers. The reception included "Live music, appetizers, buffet dinner, Champagne toast and dancing all-evening. It was a very memorable event with all of the Astroth, Conrad and Hoffmann families exchanging stories and information.

The Future Ahead

By profession I am an engineer and that has provided for my livelihood and life-style. I have ventured into business as an entrepreneur and was successful because I was fortunate to rely on my partners, employees and friends.

I intend to keep busy and continue to accept assignments as a consultant and expert witness for automotive accident cases involving child safety seats. While child restraint systems have improved greatly over the years there are issues that have not been addressed. The NHTSA FMVSS 213 & 225 Standards have not kept-up with the design and changes in the automotive industry. The auto manufacturers have not addressed child safety in the design of improved child occupancy seating positions and interior safety performance.

As an engineer dedicated to improving automotive safety, I expect to be an advocate toward promoting ideas that could address potential hazards that may exist in current and future automotive & CRS designs. Child safety systems and products that are designed for out-of-vehicle use are also regulated by the Consumer Product Safety Commission (CPSC). The cooperation between these two agencies will hopefully improve the design and performance of child safety in future products.

I am also an active Rotarian and I volunteer for charitable activities. Currently I am pursuing and promoting the production of a children's film based on my "Blue King" storybook.

Working out regularly at the Elite Fitness North health club keeps me in shape and active. I also keep busy maintaining my little vineyard and doing landscape projects. Another thing I enjoy is feeding and watching the deer, wildlife and of course the numerous feathered friends.

As I view the future I don't have any specific plans that would change my basic values and life-style. I have lived my life as events dictated that I do the right or proper thing. I have certain regrets but I also have many good memories. I am a devoted Christian and endeavor to follow the principles and values that the Lord Jesus expects of me. I have always tried to be benevolent toward others. I am happily married to Carolyn, my friend and companion.

Appendix:

Hoffmann Family Tree

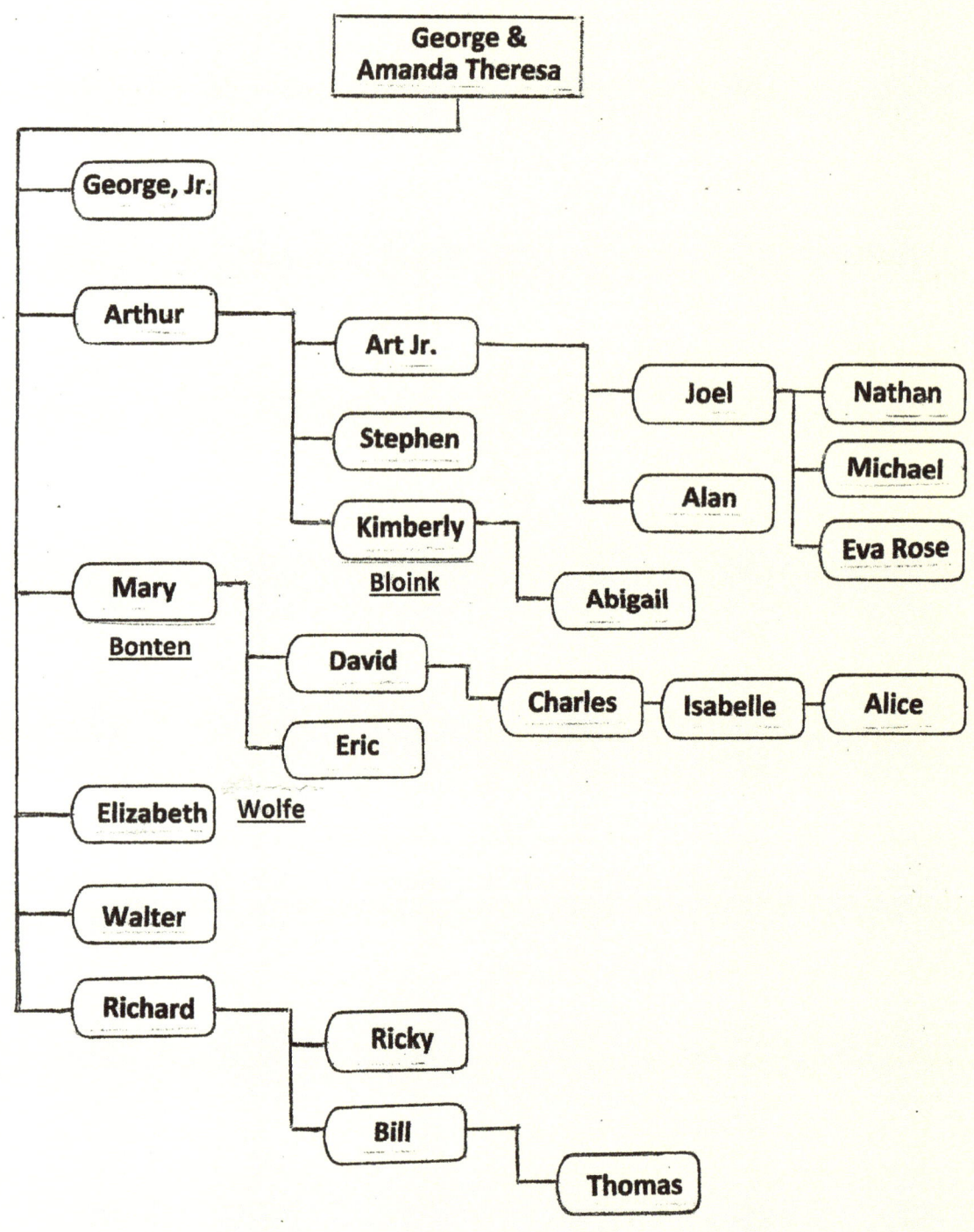

Arthur W. Hoffmann, Ed.D., P.E.

Patents and Engineering / Design Accomplishments

During my engineering career I was fortunate to work on a variety of very interesting projects in the automotive and defense/aerospace fields. My assignments were primarily in the new product design and research that offered me the opportunity to be at the forefront of developing engineering technology. I currently hold several patents related to mechanical devices and design initiatives. My primary experience is in automotive safety and this has allowed me to continue to be engaged in consulting opportunities in my private practice.

Engineering Projects / Patents / Automotive Experience

I. Patents & Applications:

1. Foam-filled automotive body structure - (bootleg pocket application)(GM).
2. GM child safety seat – features (anti-sub ramp) & (folding - feature)(GM).
3. Seat adjuster torsion-tube – mechanical crimping technology (Johnson Controls).
4. Anti-rattle seat attachment hooks (ease of assembly & eliminates fasteners)(GM).
5. Heli-screw gear application (combined one-piece spur & worm gear)(GM).
6. Energy-absorbing structural applications. (Occupant friendly interiors)(GM).
7. Fettered anti-back-out pushpin fastener. (Johnson Controls).
8. Piezo-electric linear actuator – application. (TEAM Resources).
9. Active anti-whiplash head restraint. – Application (JCI).
10. Shoulder belt height adjuster - (Chrysler, DCX).

II. Automotive Safety

1. Developed first GM child safety seat – (1st in auto industry).
2. Established initial FMVSS 201 specifications and test reqmts for interior impact.
3. GM safety seat design & development.
4. Head restraint development (1st GM headrests).
5. Anti-whiplash seat design & dynamic test development.
6. Occupant protection and passive restraint systems. (seat belts / retractors / air bags).
7. Side impact protection (GM 1st door beams).
8. Integrated seat belts to seat structure (LBTS & ABTS).
9. Dynamic impact sled and barrier test validation.
10. Review & analyses of Chrysler air bag / seat belt restraint systems test specs.
11. Design of integrated child safety restraint seat for 2nd row van/SUV seats.
12. Cargo retention system design.
13. Folding seat back lock design.
14. Seat safety development. (Headrests, rear impact, frame structure & recliners).
15. Crashworthiness – energy management / front crush initiators / hood catcher / E/A belts.

Hoffmann Incochee Estate – Traverse City, Michigan

Hoffmann – 887 Wind Drift Drive

Chãteau Du Roi Bleu